Horse
Business Management

Jeremy Houghton Brown
and
Vincent Powell-Smith

OXFORD
BSP PROFESSIONAL BOOKS
LONDON EDINBURGH BOSTON
MELBOURNE PARIS BERLIN VIENNA

Copyright © Jeremy Houghton Brown
and Ingramlight Properties Ltd 1989

BSP Professional Books
A division of Blackwell Scientific
  Publications Ltd
Editorial Offices:
Osney Mead, Oxford OX2 0EL
25 John Street, London WC1N 2BL
23 Ainslie Place, Edinburgh EH3 6AJ
3 Cambridge Center, Cambridge
  MA 02142, USA
54 University Street, Carlton
  Victoria 3053, Australia

First published 1989
Reprinted 1990 (twice), 1991

Set by DP Photosetting, Aylesbury, Bucks
Printed and bound in Great Britain by
Mackays of Chatham PLC, Chatham, Kent

DISTRIBUTORS

Marston Book Services Ltd
PO Box 87
Oxford OX2 0DT
(*Orders:* Tel: 0865 791155
         Fax: 0865 791927
         Telex: 837515)

USA
Blackwell Scientific Publications, Inc.
3 Cambridge Center
Cambridge, MA 02142
(*Orders:* Tel: (800) 759–6102)

Canada
Oxford University Press
70 Wynford Drive
Don Mills
Ontario M3C 1J9
(*Orders:* Tel: (416) 441–2941)

Australia
Blackwell Scientific Publications
(Australia) Pty Ltd
54 University Street
Carlton, Victoria 3053
(*Orders:* Tel: (03) 347–0300)

British Library
Cataloguing in Publication Data

Houghton Brown, Jeremy
  Horse business management
  1. Livestock: Horses. Management
  I. Title   II. Powell-Smith, Vincent
  636.1'083

  ISBN 0–632–02184–5

Dedication

To my sons and all my students
– theirs is the future.

JHB

For Marilyn with affection.
Proverbs 12:4

VP-S

Contents

Foreword

Many books have been written on the subject of the training and care of horses. The examination system in Britain turns out qualified instructors of varying levels well able to train and care for horses and teach pupils to ride. But their knowledge of the business side of running a horse establishment is often scant.

Now at last we have a book which informs the reader in practical terms of the pitfalls and problems of running a horse business.

Anyone who runs a small private yard needs some knowledge of business management and this book is of as much value to that person as to the proprietor of a large training establishment or equestrian centre. It is written in clear simple language which the layman can understand, and it can be read straight through or used as a reference book.

It is evident that the authors have a practical knowledge of their subject and the text is full of such common sense that it should be of benefit to all who read it.

Many people who work with horses do so because it is a vocation. They will put up with long hours and poor working conditions because they love their work. But if a yard can be well-run, efficient, and achieve its financial objectives, it will be a happier place for all concerned. If this book helps these objectives to be achieved it will be doing a great service to the horse world.

Richard Meade OBE

President of the British Equestrian Federation, former member of the British Three-Day Event Team for over twenty years, triple Olympic Gold Medallist, trainer of three-day event horses and riders, who runs an eventing and hunting yard at his home.

Preface

This book is aimed at all those who manage horses. Owners, managers, supervisors and all who make their careers with horses are investing in them; every investment can, with a little extra care and knowledge, offer greater rewards. From the one-person business to the major yard there is need for expertise and a purposeful approach that gets pleasing and successful results. This book is for those who wish to succeed. Success may be defined in terms of competitions won, a happy work place, job satisfaction, freedom from hassle, successful pupils, pride and profit.

Many people find it hard to combine their horse skills, and their caring attitude towards horses, with the different disciplines required to run a business. This book is for horse people yet it is about management. Management may be seen as a chore or a challenge but it is certainly the key to success. Good management is less stressful and more rewarding; it probably will take less time and it does not have to be complicated. Good management is about having more time and more money to do the things which give the greatest pleasure.

The aim of the book is to concentrate simply on those matters which have proved in practice to bring good results. It is a practical book for practical people. It can be used for reference when coping with problems or contemplating new ideas; it can also be used to reappraise a current business, particularly if improved profitability is sought.

All students need good books as well as good teachers and provision in the area of management has been sadly neglected until recently. Certainly this book should prove essential reading for all concerned with passing examinations be they Society examinations or National Certificates and Diplomas. Students are starting out on a career and it is to be hoped that the British Horse Industry can attract the best people and can prove worthy of those people; careers may lead into different sectors of the horse world such, as racing, studs, training centres, riding schools, trekking centres, dealers' yards and many more. In all, the principles of management, as given here, will hold good; may this book contribute to the success of all such businesses and to the success of the people who work in them.

In the text the word 'he' has been used throughout for simplicity but it is acknowledged that 'he or she' would have been more accurate or just 'she' would often have been more likely.

The authors would like to acknowledge and thank all who have advised on and contributed to this book including family, friends, colleagues and students; also to thank all who have over the years provided both the theory and the practice on which this book is based. Particular thanks are due to Mrs Wendy Garratt for her help in typing the manuscript.

1 Horses: a business and an industry

The horse industry and its organisations

'Horses' and 'industry' are not a contradiction in terms. An industry is a branch of commercial enterprise concerned with the output of a specified product or service. It is an organised economic activity, and in this sense the horse industry is a significant one in the United Kingdom. Because those who work with horses are not grouped into factories, found on industrial estates or located in the high street, it is easy to underestimate their number. The horse industry is fragmented but is a major employer of labour, though its identity and significance is often overlooked. This may be because of the small size and variety of the various individual units of which it is comprised.

Agriculture, in contrast, has long been accepted as a major industry. Successive governments have assigned Ministers to watch over and help it, while the horse industry is left largely to fend for itself, despite the fact that, other than farming, it is the largest land-based industry; others are forestry, horticulture and fish-farming. However, the tide turned in 1987 when Mr Ted Smith, speaking for the Government, said: 'There has been a change in policy; we now see a significant role for horses and intend to assist'. The following year the British Horse Society published a major report on the size of the British horse industry. It showed that there are:

- about half a million horses and ponies;
- three million regular riders;
- a total annual turnover of £760 million;
- £50 million exports;
- 800,000 hectares of land used for horses.

It is possible to classify industries in many ways, ranging from numbers employed, capital employed, turnover, land use, foreign currency earnings to contribution in terms of pleasure or product. The horse industry scores highly under all these heads. Recent figures suggest that there are about 50,000 people working directly with horses as either employees or on a self-employed basis, but taking into account those indirectly involved – who range from farriers to bookmakers – this figure can be trebled. Indeed, in a House of Commons debate in 1984 it was stated that between 150,000 and 250,000 people were employed in the horse industry in its wider sense. Figure 1.1 is based on several sources including the British Horse Society survey. Variations in the figures are due to seasonality, part-time workers and trainees.

The horse industry also has a diffuse image because it is divided into three parts:

- the racing industry;
- the non-thoroughbred industry;
- horse-associated activities.

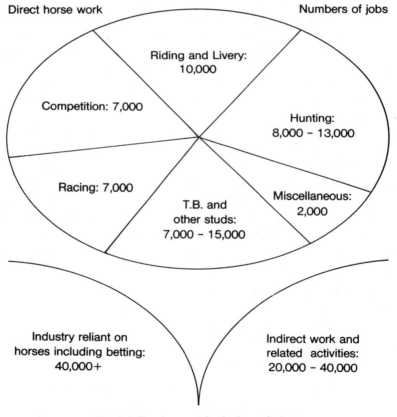

Fig. 1.1 Employment in the horse industry.

The racing industry

The racing industry consists of breeding, rearing, buying and selling, and the training and racing of thoroughbred horses. It is sometimes called the thoroughbred industry and is divided into flat racing and National Hunt racing 'over the sticks'. It has a high profile and an enormous following. The horses are valuable and the prizes are large. The lucrative side of racing is flat racing, when young horses are trained to race as two and three year olds. They may then be retired to stud, be culled or, more rarely, will stay in racing. There is a high wastage rate and of the mares going to a stallion, less than half will achieve progeny which become race horses. The average two year old only races twice, and the average three year old only three times. It is a tough business and behind the glamour of the racecourse lie high risks.

National Hunt racing is divided into steeplechasing, hurdling and hunter chasing, of which steeplechasing and hurdling provide the majority of business for professional trainers. It is also a hard business, as it takes place through the autumn, winter and spring. Although the horses are tough and mature, they are subjected to the great stress of big jumps, high speeds, heavy weights and ground that may be deep or hard.

The Jockey Club is the governing body responsible for controlling flat racing and steeplechasing in Britain and issues one rule book to govern both. It is the ruling body of the sport and has wide powers of discipline, including power to fine a trainer or jockey or to withdraw or suspend a licence to train or ride. The Jockey Club also lays down regulations for point-to-pointing, which is the amateur version of steeplechasing.

The breeding of racehorses is co-ordinated by the Thoroughbred Breeders Association, founded in 1917. Its objects are to encourage and ensure co-operative effort in all matters pertaining to the production and improvement of thoroughbred horses and the interests of their breeders.

Trainers come together under the National Trainers' Association, which was formed to protect the interests of flat racing trainers. Stable lads (of both sexes) have a choice between the Stable Lads' Association or the Racing and Equestrian Section of the Agricultural and Allied Workers National Trade Group within the Transport and General Workers' union.

Arab racing is another side of the racing industry. It is quite separate from flat and National Hunt racing, and is increasing in popularity. Driving racing is also distinct but has not yet achieved a great following in Britain; it is a major sport throughout many other parts of Europe.

The non-thoroughbred industry

This is the largest section of the horse industry since it covers all others who have horses and ponies. It can be divided in various ways, such as breeders and users, but this is not really very helpful. The most logical method of classification is by organisations.

The largest and oldest part of this sector is Hunting. The majority of packs of hounds hunt the fox (a few foxes are hunted on foot in mountain country). There are also harriers which hunt the hare (beagles also hunt hares but with both Hunt staff and followers on foot) and buck hounds and stag hounds hunt deer. Hunt followers subscribe to individual Hunts. The Masters of Foxhounds Association (MFHA), founded in 1881, stands in some respects in the same position to fox-hunting as the Jockey Club does to racing, but there is an important difference between the two organisations. The MFHA deals only with Masters of Foxhounds and committees of recognised Hunts; it has no control over individual fox-hunters. A recognised Hunt is one which has been officially accepted by the Committee of the MFHA and whose name is recorded on the official list of recognised Hunts.

Individual hunting folk belong to the British Field Sports Society, which is a strong and active body representative of all country sports and not merely of hunting.

Pleasure riders may well belong to a local Riding Club, which will probably be affiliated to the British Horse Society (BHS), which was founded in 1947 by the amalgamation of older organisations and which is now the authority and parent body of all horse and pony interests in Great Britain. Younger riders may well belong to their local branch of the Pony Club, which is also part of the BHS. Usually, each Pony Club is named after the local Hunt and has strong connections with it, but there are also urban branches of the Pony Club in areas where there is no hunt.

Many people who ride each week do not have their own horse or pony and rely for their mounts on the local riding school. These establishments have to be licensed by the local authority, but may also be affiliated to the BHS and/or the Association of British Riding Schools (ABRS). Both of these organisations have a system of examinations for both pleasure and career riders. The National Pony Society (NPS), founded in 1893, also has an examination structure and offers training and qualifications in stud management. The NPS takes particular responsibility for Britain's native breeds. Show ponies, which are based on native breeds crossed with thoroughbred and Arab blood, are the concern of the British Show Pony Society. It is the controlling body for improving and regulating the showing of children's riding ponies. A third national pony society – the Ponies Association (UK) (formerly Ponies of Britain) – is particularly associated with showing and trecking. The BHS also takes an interest in trekking, and there are other associations such as the Pony Trekking and Riding Society of Wales and the Scottish Trekking and Riding Association.

Another major group within the non-thoroughbred sector consists of competitive riders who are divided into various disciplines. In terms of both popularity and television coverage, show jumping is the most important competitive discipline. Clubs and Riding Schools organise jumping at local level, but the more serious contests are affiliated to the British Show Jumping Association (BSJA) which is the controlling body of show jumping in Great Britain. The BSJA is represented at international level by the British Equestrian Federation (BEF), which also represents the British Horse Society in international arrangements for dressage, horse trials, driving and long-distance riding. The BHS has separate groups for each of these sports. The British Driving Society is a specialist association for those interested in the driving of horses and ponies. There is also the Horse and Pony Endurance Society. The International Equestrian Federation (Federation Equestré Internationale) governs the sport of riding on an international basis. It consists of representatives of the affiliated national bodies.

Polo stands alone as a sport, and is governed by the Hurlingham Polo Association which has jurisdiction over the game.

Competing includes showing, and every breed of horse has its own breed society. Various national bodies are concerned with breeds or types. These include the British Show Hack and Cob Society, which was founded in 1938 to further the interests of owners and breeders of hacks and cobs; the National Light Horse Breeding Society, founded in 1885 to improve the breed and promote the breeding of hunters and other riding horses; and the British Warm Blood Society founded in 1980.

The thousands of horse and pony owners who merely ride for pleasure also form part of the non-thoroughbred sector. Many of them belong to the British Horse Society which tries to care for their interests. The final – and an important – group are disabled people who benefit in many ways from contact with horses. The Riding for the Disabled Association (RDA) was formed as a charity in 1969 to encourage riding for the physically and mentally disabled. Regional groups have been formed throughout the United Kingdom as well as in continental Europe.

The Equestrian Section of the Agricultural and Allied Workers Trade Group which is part of the Transport and General Workers' Union is active in offering a trades union for all who work with horses. Its parent body offers a trades union for many who work in the horse-associated activities.

Horse-associated activities

The third sector of the horse industry consists of all those who rely on horses for a living. These associated activities include:

- veterinary surgeons;
- farriers and blacksmiths;
- auctioneers;
- knackers;
- saddlers and loriners;
- feed compounders and merchants;
- insurers and insurance agents;
- tack shops and horse clothiers;
- showground and racetrack staff;
- bookmakers and betting shops;
- horse society staff;
- sporting tailors and outfitters;
- bootmakers and hatters;
- journalists and publishers;
- cart and carriage makers;
- horsebox and trailer makers;
- stabling manufacturers and builders;
- hauliers and transporters;
- hunt staff;
- college staff;

and many others.

There are many specialist organisations representative of these various interests. These include, for example, the British Equine Veterinary Association, the Farriers Registration Council and the Society of Master Saddlemakers. There are related livery companies of the City of London such as the Worshipful Company of Loriners, the Worshipful Company of Saddlers and the Worshipful Company of Farriers.

An overall trade association is the British Equestrian Trade Association which holds trade fairs and publishes an excellent Directory covering the whole of the horse industry and providing up-to-date names,

- Manager, administrator, executive secretary
- Sales, marketing, technical and advisory officers
- Equestrian centre manager
- Stud manager, bloodstock agent
- Journalist, media work
- Public relations, communications
- Lecturer, instructor, coach
- Dealer, livery yard manager
- Stabling, transport, tack
- Health care, consultant
- Trainer, head girl, groom
- Rider, racing lad, driving

Fig. 1.2 Some jobs in the horse industry.

addresses and telephone numbers, as well as an annual review of changes affecting the industry.

Because the Horse Industry is so diverse, ambitious school leavers now can consider a broader list of possible horse careers than was formerly the case (Fig. 1.2).

Training and education

In the early 1980s, the Government appointed a committee under the chairmanship of Charles Ansell to investigate training and education leading to qualifications in the land-based industries. Its report (Report of the National Consultative Group for the Co-ordination of Validating Arrangements in Agriculture and Related Subjects) was published in 1985. The Government initiative brought together the various horse associations concerned with training, and it was agreed to progress Ansell's recommendations before the publication of the final report. In 1983, a Working Group for Training and Education for work with horses was set up under the chairmanship of the late Dorian Williams. The Group set out to produce a ladder of skills for those seeking a career with horses, and published this as *Levels of Horse Care and Management*, Book 1 (1985) and Book 2 (1986). The principal authors were the late Pat Smallwood and Jeremy Houghton Brown; John Goldsmith of the BHS co-ordinated the work. Subsequently, the Group produced a *Directory of Career Training in the Horse Industry*. The Group's final task was to prepare the way for the Horse Council.

The Joint National Horse Education and Training Council (JNHETC) was formed in 1987 to provide a forum for consultation between

Fig. 1.3 The logo of the Joint National Horse Education and Training Council (JNHETC).

Government, industry, education and training bodies on all aspects of education and training in the horse industry. Its logo is shown in Fig. 1.3. The JNHETC was formed just at the right time because the Government launched a programme of National Vocational Qualifications which required every industry to form its own 'lead body' and establish its own system of 'levels'. The horse industry was the only one in the country to have anticipated the need and to have already met both of these requirements.

The 'levels' are not examination syllabuses, but form a common standard available to all the examining bodies dealing with horses. To meet national requirements, the levels have to be expressed in a particular format which shows both the skills and the criteria for judging performance. In due course, all career qualifications awarded by all organisations will also be credited as National Vocational Qualifications (NVQ). This should lead to:

> 'development of a better trained, competent, qualified workforce; increased co-operation between employers, training organisations and awarding bodies; increased individual motivation and awareness of standards on the part of employees and easier identification and recruitment of competent staff'.

To meet NVQ requirements examinations will be taken in units, bit by bit, and many will be tested at the workplace and not at an examination centre.

The JNHETC (the Horse Council), then, is responsible for all aspects of training and education in the horse industry. It is recognised by the Training Commission as a 'non-statutory training organisation' and 'industry-led body'. It has sub-committees covering Youth Training, Courses and Locations, Tests and Examinations and Heavy Horse Training. Much of its work has been in establishing new levels for the National Council for Vocational Qualifications (NCVQ).

In future each horse-related examining body will probably have its awards double-stamped to show that its qualifications are in line with the requirements of the Horse Council (JNHETC) and with National Standards (NCVQ).

The main horse organisations offering examinations are the British Horse Society, the Association of British Riding Schools and the National Pony Society. Two other national bodies are also concerned and these validate the college exams – the Business and Technician Education Council (BTEC) and the National Examinations Board for Agriculture, Horticulture and Allied Industries (NEBAHAI). BTEC caters for those who are attending Agricultural or Technical Colleges for two or three years in order to gain a Diploma or Higher Diploma. Students working for NEBAHAI examinations attend College for one year in order to gain a Certificate, or Advanced Certificate but the NEBAHAI also acts as an examining body for those taking part in some Youth Training Scheme (YTS). The professional horse management qualifications are shown in Fig. 1.4.

The one and two year YTS (more properly called Training for Skills) is a recognised route of entry for a career in the horse industry. The Industry Preferred Training Pattern (IPTP) is agreed between the Training Commission and the Horse Council and is based on the 'Levels of Horse Care and Management'.

YTS is a scheme designed to prepare those leaving school for the world of work and is available to those of 16 and 17 years of age. It combines working in a yard for a 'work experience provider' (WEP), with attendance at a College or Training Centre on a day release or block release basis. Trainees are encouraged to take examinations which lead to recognised qualifications. The scheme is organised locally by Approved Training Organisations (formerly Managing Agents).

An advantage of YTS as a system of formal training is that it is monitored by all sides of industry to ensure that employers (as work experience providers) adhere to the conditions of the scheme. It is not intended to be a form of cheap labour. YTS is government-sponsored and is operated by the Training Commission through Approved Training

Levels		Societies				Examination bodies (college-based exams)	
Old levels of horse care and management	New NVQ Levels	British Horse Society Horsemastership	BHS Teaching	Association of British Riding Schools	National Pony Society	National Examining Board for Agriculture Horticulture and Allied Industries	Business and Technician Education Council (BTEC)
1	–	Horse Knowledge and Riding I	–	Preliminary Horse Care and Riding I	Stud Trainee Certificate Part I	Phase I Horse Husbandry (discontinued 1990)	–
2 Trainee	1	Horse Knowledge and Riding II	–	Prelim. Horse Care and Riding II	Stud Trainee Certificate Part II	Phase II Changing to NVQ 1	–
3 Competent	2	Horse Knowledge Riding III	Prelim. Teaching Certificate	Assistant Groom Certificate	Stud Assistant Certificate	National Certificate in the Management of Horses	BTEC General and Business Studies (Horse) Diploma
		ASSISTANT INSTRUCTOR					
4 Supervisor	3	Horse Knowledge and Riding IV	Intermediate Teaching Cert.	Groom's Diploma	Stud Diploma	Advanced National Certificate in Equine Business Management	BTEC Horse Studies and Management Diploma
		INTERMEDIATE INSTRUCTOR					
Manager	4	Stable Management Certificate Equitation + Teaching		Riding School Principal's Diploma	Stud Manager's Diploma	–	BTEC Higher National Diploma in Horse Studies (Management and Technology)
		INSTRUCTOR					

Fig. 1.4 Professional horse management qualifications.

Notes:
(1) It may be appropriate to take more than one qualification at any level. In the future, under NVQ, any common elements between the two exams will not need to be re-examined.
(2) The college-based exams at any level tend to include in the course of study considerable preparation for the next level up.

Organisations which are responsible for organising the 'off-the-job' training days.

The trainee receives a weekly allowance from the ATO and this is payable even when the trainee is on holiday. The WEP is expected to make a financial contribution. The trainee works a 40 hour week. Overtime is not compulsory, but if performed by the trainee must be paid for at a realistic rate. The trainee is entitled to 26 days' holiday each year. These conditions came as something of a shock to many people engaged in the horse industry where, on the thoroughbred side, the working week is about 40 to 46 hours, and on the non-thoroughbred side is typically between 50 and 60 hours.

Initial training and education is the right way to start a career and leads to jobs and ongoing education and training. The horse industry has yet to achieve a clear career structure with good opportunities for the most able. To some extent, this exists in the thoroughbred sector, but the lack of such a structure on the non-thoroughbred side leads to an enormous wastage of young people leaving the industry and to a shortage of well-qualified and experienced staff. The developments now taking place at national level should do much to combat this.

Choice of enterprise and management style

There are many types of business within the horse industry, and within each business there may be several different enterprises. An enterprise in this sense is a unit within the business as a whole – a riding school may offer livery as well as buying and selling horses and ponies. The difficulty lies not so much in the choice of enterprise, but in deciding why that enterprise is a sensible venture. Many horse businesses continue for years without any reappraisal of the situation, and many people start a horse business without reviewing all the possibilities.

Selecting the right enterprise calls for self-examination about one's motives and ambitions. 'What am I seeking to achieve in my life?' is the sort of question to be answered. An honest answer would in general be a mixture of 'Take pride in all I do', 'Achieve something worthwhile' and 'Follow my star'!

A love of animals may give one the ambition to become a veterinary surgeon, but despite hard work and good motivation, the necessary exceptional 'A' level grades may not be achieved. Such a person might find a closely-related career with animals satisfying and rewarding, perhaps in the horse industry. Another person who was attracted to horses may have spent most of their spare time riding, caring for horses or perhaps even just thinking about them, but performed badly in school examinations, left as soon as possible, and then embarked on a career with horses. Thus people come into the industry by different routes, and in due course come to the point of deciding what enterprise they wish to manage or business they wish to create. The basic criteria are straightforward. One should concentrate on what one does best. The criterion of pride is more demanding; it may seek profit for a desired lifestyle; it may seek success in competition or through reputation. Satisfying it will require that the chosen business is well-run and is profitable.

To achieve these objectives requires an amalgam of wise decisions: good location, suitable aims and good management.

There are many styles of management, and these are best considered separately. The management of a business is shown in Fig. 1.5.

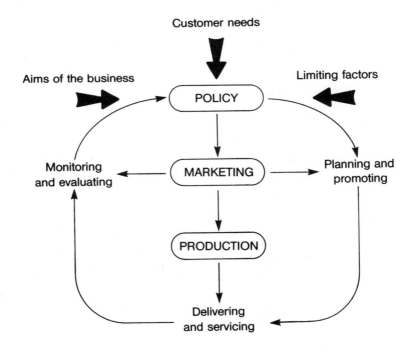

Of the three main management responsibilities, Policy, Marketing and Production, many horse businesses concentrate on the third almost to the exclusion of the other two and greatly to the detriment of the business

Fig. 1.5 The management of a business.

Management by objectives

In a large company, the board of directors usually establishes a long-term plan and short-term objectives, and the company's performance is monitored. Where there has been under-performance, the underlying reasons will be analysed and the plan reviewed. If good performance is achieved, the success is analysed and new targets are set. Long-term objectives will change in the light of the political and financial climates, the activities of competitors, and technological and other changes.

A sales company, for example, will have a national sales target, which will be divided into regional figures which regional sales managers are realistically expected to achieve. The regions will be divided into areas with each area manager having a target, and in turn the individual salesmen's targets will be set. The company's overall objective is thus divided and each individual is under pressure to help to achieve it. Bonuses may be offered to individuals and all those involved have a corporate desire to achieve their individual targets.

Few businesses in the horse industry set such specific targets; pipe-dreams seem to be more the order of the day. But successful businesses do set objectives. A riding school might set the target of achieving a 20 per cent increase in the number of lessons given by a stated date. A stud could plan to achieve a 15 per cent higher price for its yearlings than was the case the previous year.

Targets can be published and discussed, but they must be realistic targets and the management must be able to persuade the staff that this is the case. A riding school teacher might, for example, say that she could attract more clients if only the school was not so dusty, the noise of passing traffic did not drown her instruction or if parents did not get so cold while waiting. These are long-standing and well-known problems at the school, but with a set target and staff involvement, the teacher's problems are clearly identified as the stumbling blocks to the achievement of the objective. In this light, possible solutions can be costed and the costs compared against the likely or possible increase in business.

If a manager is to achieve the owner's objectives, these must be spelt out and given a time-scale. A manager's hardest task is often to find out exactly what the owner wants from the business. The honest answer may be that the owner wants to give the business to his daughter five years hence as a thriving concern. At first sight, such an answer might be thought to demotivate the manager, but in fact he should be delighted to face such a clear-cut challenge to his ability. In five years time, the business should be so buoyant and have such high standards and well-trained staff that its new owner can take over. The business would maintain the manager's style and the staff would have the continuing pleasure of working in a happy and prosperous environment. With such success behind him, the manager would find other establishments clamouring for his services if the new owner wished to manage the concern herself and had the ability to do so.

If the owner or manager is to keep the policy for the business up to date he must consider the following options:

(a) What future changes may occur to the situation?
   What are the probabilities?
   What would be the consequences?

(b) What are the business's strengths?
   What are its weaknesses?
   What savings could be made?
   What new projects or enterprises could be created?

Management for quality

It is not easy to make a profit from running a horse business. Many horse businesses are family concerns which utilise the home and the time of all the family to achieve pleasure but not much profit. Others start out in high hopes and with a heavy mortgage, but the competition is too stiff and the owners quit the struggle. But in every area of the country there tends to be a horse business – stud, livery yard or riding school – which becomes *the* place to go to from the clients' point of view. Usually, the common factor is *quality*. Achieving it is not simply a matter of decision by the owners. Quality is only achieved by getting commitment from staff and this means offering them responsibility. Overall commitment to quality and the achievement of set objectives is clearly demonstrated by Japanese industrial companies which adopt a 'total team' approach to success, and the same principles can be applied to any business.

Staff and clients alike enjoy associating with a business which has a reputation for quality. Pride and morale rise. People like to do things well. Quality involves a commitment to the clients and the more a business commits itself to clients, the more they will commit themselves to the business. As one successful event rider said: 'When I need a new young horse I always go back to the same dealer. Although I have to pay a little more for the horse, over the years I have always found it good value'.

Management by organisation

Any business, however small, must have an organisation. Yet some businesses appear to be organised chaos. At one riding school, for example, when sufficient clients have arrived at the yard, they go with their instructor to catch their horses. Lessons are held in open fields amongst grazing horses. The horses are turned loose afterwards, the clients pay the instructor in cash, which he places in an urn in the hall of the owner's house. The local farmer delivering hay is paid from the same urn.

Generally a horse business will have a clear chain of command but if they are only commands dissatisfaction will ensue. The better characteristics to look for are specialisation in particular jobs which are ongoing posts in that business so suitably qualified individuals can be recruited; thus the business has or trains up the best people for the jobs. Secondly the hierarchy of authority is clear and includes responsibility at every level. Dissatisfaction is inevitable if the head lad gives an order and two minutes later the trainer arrives in the yard and countermands that order. Such problems are particularly prevalent when there is an owning family and a manager: the poor manager finds his staff getting conflicting orders from different members of the family.

It follows that the organisation must have rules; rules for safety are obvious, though sometimes overlooked. Rules about agreed procedures are essential. Some procedures may be complex, e.g. those in case of fire, while others are simple routines such as how a stranger is to be greeted if found in the yard. Some rules must be worked out carefully; for example, agreement with the vet and the stud groom as to the procedure for the person sitting up when a mare goes into labour.

Another characteristic of a successful organisation is that the format is not built around individual personality and preference but around achieving the agreed set objectives. Individual personalities can be a wonderful asset and it would be foolish to ignore special skills, but a successful business does not organise about these as key factors.

The formal organisation of a business is not bureaucratic and impersonal. A carefully-defined and orderly organisation allows for equality of treatment because it is rational. The problem is one of balance. The organisation should not be inflexible, neither should it be so formal that loyalty is lost.

In larger companies lines of responsibility are often based on what is called 'the rule of five'. This states that no person should be responsible for or supervise any more than five direct subordinates. Thus, the owner of a riding school may have up to five key people each charged with responsibility for an area: the Yard Manager, the Chief Instructor, the Secretary, and the Estate man, for example. Under some of these there may be a team of up to five assistants. The important point is that each individual must know to whom they are responsible and whom they should approach in case of doubt or difficulty. The key concept is a team which cares for the job and whose members care for each other.

The manager receives the highest remuneration because his decisions are crucial to the success or failure of the operation. When reaching a decision, good managers sound out the team and explain the position. Staff in general appreciate a manager's right to manage, but they also appreciate being kept in the picture. Good communications are a priority and must be built into the work routine and become a second habit. There must always be a time and place when staff can find out what is going on.

Managers have key responsibilities in the areas of administration, production and marketing. The last named is the area most commonly neglected in the horse world.

Management for profit

Profit is one of the most obvious but elusive indicators of success in managing a horse business. Professionals who are concerned with this aspect of the business include the bank manager and accountant whose livelihoods are largely provided by successful businesses.

The first essential is to know how the business is doing financially at present so that the true financial picture can be assessed. It is also useful to compare the position with that of other businesses of similar scope and size. Those who invest in a business – its owners and possibly relatives as well as the bank – wish to know the return on their investment. A financial health-check of this kind shows up any areas of weakness.

If changes are planned, they must be budgeted for. Good records are essential, and the importance of proper financial management cannot be overstressed. Finance and profit are discussed in Chapter 5.

Marketing

Market-orientated management is probably the unrecognised philosophy behind many successful horse businesses. Marketing has been defined as 'producing a product that does not come back for customers who do' and is as much applicable to horse businesses as to any other.

Marketing activities are:

- identifying the customer requirement;
- gearing the business to satisfy the requirement and making a profit;
- reacting to change in customers' needs so that the business continues to be profitable;
- advertising and selling.

The product may be a horse, a breeding policy, a stallion at stud, a clipping service, a livery business – in fact, anything relating to horses.

A marketing campaign

Successful marketing requires a campaign. The elements of a campaign are easy to identify:

(1) *Find the idea*. This entails research by reading about new developments, attending conferences and visiting leading establishments. In this way one finds the market opportunity.
(2) *Consider the market*. Analyse the market and potential competition as well as the cost factors.
(3) *Prepare a plan*. In some cases it may be possible to run a pilot scheme or a test marketing exercise. Many possibilities are rejected at this stage.
(4) *Prepare for implementation*. An advertising and public relations campaign may be initiated and the media involved.
(5) *Launch the product*. Selling is an essential part of any business, but the entrepreneur must ensure that the necessary back-up can be provided.
(6) *Monitor on-going performance*, including quality control. Performance monitoring extends to advertising as well.

Experience is a learning process and may mean changes in plans. There must be an awareness of changing market needs and a willingness to adapt.

Other considerations include the owner's ambitions, staff competence, training and needs, as well as the activities of competitors. There may be various limiting factors too, such as locality or space.

Advertising

Advertising requires a systematic approach. It must be based on research so that it is properly aimed and takes any competition into account. The benefits of the product must be listed and placed in order of importance so that the 'advertising message' is clear. A campaign is then prepared to a budget and the advertisements are drafted. A good advertisement meets four criteria of the acronym AIDA:

- Attracts attention.
- Interest is aroused.
- Desire is created.
- Action is stimulated.

A good advertisement thus catches the reader's eye and is immediately interesting. The message stimulates a desire for the product. A good advertisement should also stimulate immediate action, which accounts for some of the success of mail-order selling.

Promotions

Public relations is an important aspect of any business. It starts with first impressions when a telephone enquiry is made. The first impression is based on the way in which the telephone is answered and the call is dealt with. Similarly, a prompt response to a letter and good notepaper suggest

Fig. 1.6 A new stable yard calls for a grand opening. Here the Saddlers Stable Yard at Stoneleigh receives a royal visit watched by the National Coach and the Centre Manager/ Complex Designer.

quality, style and efficiency. Every business should develop a 'house style' covering every detail: the notice boards, the colour of the stable doors, notepaper, advertisements and press releases.

A new product may call for a launch combining several methods of promotion. A typical launch will have a guest speaker or celebrity to open the new building, welcome the new stallion or whatever. Media representatives and other guests will be invited and the budget must include refreshments. A press release should be prepared and distributed to the equestrian and local press and to local radio and television. The publicity obtained in this way can be far more effective than paid advertisements, but normally a campaign will combine both methods.

There are also opportunities for direct mail. Local equestrian organisations may be prepared to include a leaflet in their mailing to members in return for a contribution towards postage. Relevant directories and trade lists (as well as the Yellow Pages of the Telephone Directory) can form the basis of lists for direct mail. With new products aimed nationally, specialist promotion companies can be used, though their charges tend to be expensive.

A trade stand at a local show can pay dividends and attract new

Fig. 1.7 Success in the show ring can increase the value of young stock sold from the stud; also it publicises and increases the value of the stallions.

customers The exact nature and extent of the promotion will depend on the type of enterprise.

Care with the entry in the Telephone Directory, the Yellow Pages and Thompsons Directory is important. For riding schools and trekking centres a brochure or card can be placed in local leisure centres, inns, restaurants, libraries, hotels, guest houses and so on; also tourist information publications offer good possibilities. Showing is an important way of promoting a stud (Fig. 1.7). Stallions can be paraded at local shows and point-to-points. Competing, providing it is successful, is also useful and the horsebox acts as a publicity medium. Going hunting is an important means of making contacts in any area.

In summary, successful management requires clear objectives, quality, efficient organisation, proper financial control and good marketing. The entrepreneur should check his business regularly against these criteria.

2 Premises

The site

The right location is important for any business and many factors must be taken into account when choosing a site. In many cases, there is no option of choice, since the site is already an established one. However, the considerations guiding someone who has the choice of location for a new horse enterprise are just as useful to those with an established business or for whom the location is already fixed.

Local topography is important – accessibility, centres of population, available resources and possible future developments are all factors which should be taken into account. For example, if the business is to be based on the giving of hourly riding lessons, by allowing for the quality of the lessons and the riders' level of expertise, the number of potential clients can be predicted. Beginners and those being instructed on a weekly basis will not wish to travel too far. In all probability, they will not drive past another riding school offering a similar service unless there is a strong incentive to do so.

Thus, when considering the suitability of premises for such a business, important questions are 'Where are the clients?'; 'How easy is it for them to get to lessons?'; and 'Where is the competition?'. Most riding schools need a nearby town in order to be successful. A business based on day-treks throughout the year will, in contrast, need three urban centres within an hour's drive.

As the product on offer becomes more specialised, people will travel further; a top-class dressage trainer may attract customers willing to travel an hour or more for a single lesson. If the enterprise is a stud standing several stallions, the questions must be 'Where are the mare owners?' and 'What other stallions are at stud in the district?' Owners will bring a mare a long way to the right stallion, but they appreciate a location convenient to the motorway network for fast and easy travel. A racehorse trainer must look to where his potential patrons live; ideally,

Fig. 2.1 A modern complex in Southern England built for a royal Arab owner.

this should not be too close but should be within range of visiting the stables. Racing stables need to be convenient to several racecourses and must be well served by major roads if the horses are to race further afield regularly.

After access, competition and customers, it is important to investigate the facilities available in the area. A trekking business needs bridleways that link up to create a variety of day treks. A racing trainer will need gallops. Most horse activities benefit from quiet country lanes with wide grass verges. People getting horses fit, whether for hunting or competition, will need a few hills. Show jumpers should study the locations of the bigger indoor schools which are part of the winter show-jumping circuit.

However, it is important to look to the future. A proposed motorway coming close by will push up the value of a property dramatically, but one coming too close will depress its value and possibly cause cessation of business. Purchasing a property convenient to a famous dressage trainer is splendid for the dressage rider until the trainer moves away and his property is bought by a show jumping trainer! An area that seems to be crying out for a good riding school may seem an excellent place to buy a smallholding suitable for conversion – until one discovers, after buying the property, that a nearby farmer has obtained planning permission to convert his beef-fattening complex into a riding school. He has not only land and buildings which are easily convertible to stables and an indoor school, but may possibly have grant aid to establish his new business. Some of these problems are imponderable; others can be avoided by making local enquiries before agreeing to buy.

Soil type is also important for equine businesses. Ideally, the soil should be free-draining so as to allow some horses to be wintered out with consequent savings in labour and bedding. The free draining soils are generally those with a higher percentage of sand when compared with clay. They are generally called light soils or light land, not because of their weight but because they could be worked with a lighter team of horses. Loam – a mixture of sand, silt and clay – is what to look for. Heavier land, which is mostly clay, drains less well and so tends to get poached in winter and thus will not take horses from Christmas until it dries out in late spring. Heavy clay soils – even with drains – get deep and muddy in winter. Even in summer, heavier land can be difficult as, during a dry spell, it sets rock-hard and cracks. Farmers like heavier soils because they are more fertile and grow better crops, whereas light land is not only less productive but is also feels the effects of drought more quickly and so may run short of grass in midsummer.

Land prices are another factor to be considered when selecting an area. In areas of high employment and prosperity, land tends to be more expensive than in less affluent areas. Hill land is cheaper than prime arable or pasture land. Milk and corn are the two main profit sources for most British farms and so land which is suitable only for beef and sheep will cost less. However, the initial price is only part of the picture. In many cases it will be more prudent to take a bigger mortgage on a more expensive property than to buy a cheap property with a low earning potential. Land prices rose rapidly for a decade, peaking in 1984, and then, due to decreasing farm profitability, steadied on a plateau. Rents followed a similar pattern but now are declining. Term dates for tenancies vary with area and type of farming; common dates are Candlemas (2 February) Lady Day (25 March) and Michaelmas (29 September).

Planning and Building Regulations permission

Where there is already an established commercial horse business on a property, planning permission is probably unnecessary. However, this is one of the things that a solicitor should check when acting for a purchaser. Planning permission is needed for any 'development' and this includes what the planners call 'a material change of use', even if no building work is needed to carry out the change of use. Thus, planning permission will be required if private stabling is to be turned into a riding school or other commercial enterprise. Similarly, under the present law, if the established use is farming, planning permission will be needed if the use is to be changed to that of a horse business. Forms can be obtained from the local district council. If planning permission is refused at local level, the planning authority should tell you why and you may discuss the reasons with them and find out if their objections can be overcome. There is a right to appeal to the Secretary of State for the Environment, which may involve a public inquiry. If planning permission is required, it is sensible to engage the services of a local architect or chartered surveyor.

The planning authority's concerns are as follows:

- the provision of development plans for their area;
- the suitability of the site (and whether an alternative site may be available);
- the impact on the character or amenity value of the area;
- any employment considerations (show these as benefits);
- implications for volume and type of traffic, access and road safety;
- drainage and the burden on mains water and sewerage;
- appearance and materials used;
- effects on wildlife and landscape;
- noise, pollution and other nuisance.

Merely using land for grazing horses is regarded as an agricultural use and so planning permission is unnecessary. Individual private householders are also able to carry out certain 'permitted developments' without making an application for planning permission: erecting a stable or loose box is permitted and is regarded as the enlargement of the house itself. However, neither of these concessions is of much assistance to someone wishing to operate a horse business, and the question of planning permission (or lack of it) is an important factor when making a decision whether or not to acquire a property. An existing planning permission may lay down special conditions, and in National Parks, areas of outstanding natural beauty and conservation areas, there may be special restrictions.

Even if planning permission exists or is granted, building regulations approval if any structural work or work involving a change in the use of the premises is to be undertaken subject to minor exceptions, e.g.

Fig. 2.2 Old premises suitable for conversion to private houses with stables now fetch high prices in many areas.

approval is not needed to erect a small detached building of less than 30 square metres floor area, with no sleeping accommodation, such as a garden shed. The building regulations are administered by the building control officers of the district councils, from whom the appropriate forms are obtained. If unauthorised work is carried out, the district council can require its removal or alteration, but in practice if more than a year has elapsed since the work was completed, there is little they can do. Obtaining approval under the building regulations is not as difficult as obtaining planning permission, and local building control officers are generally most helpful.

Anyone intending to carry on the business of keeping horses either for the purpose of letting them out on hire and/or giving riding instruction for payment will require a Riding Establishment Licence from the district council. The present position in England, Wales and Scotland is governed by the Riding Establishments Acts 1964 and 1970, and is explained in Chapter 4. The law is now under review and there is a lobby seeking to introduce changes such as raising the minimum age of those left in charge of the establishment and possibly of extending the legislation to include livery stables.

Suitability

When considering the purchase of an existing horse business, it is important to find out why the business is for sale. There may be a straightforward reason such as retirement or moving from the area or purchasing another enterprise. On the other hand, it may be that the seller has failed to make a profit. If this is so, there are two problems. First, the business may not be viable – at least in its present form. Second, the establishment may have earned itself a poor reputation. That may be more of a hindrance than having no reputation at all.

Working out whether premises are suitable is not an easy task. It requires a great deal of hard work in terms of planning, budgeting and costing. Even if the business can be established within one's available and procurable finances, there are still risks because the number of clients and the profitability of the business are largely conjectural in the case of a new business. Indeed, even when purchasing an established business with existing clients as a 'going concern' the same problem must be faced.

In some cases, one already has suitable premises to hand. The question then is 'Should we operate a horse business here and, if so, what sort of horse business should it be?' This question is not easy to answer, but experienced advice is available from various bodies. The government offers help through the Agricultural Development and Advisory Service (ADAS) (The Head Office is at Great Westminster House, Horseferry Road, London SW1P 2AE). The advice is not free, but the ADAS service offers good value for money, especially about problems which are similar to those in agriculture such as buildings, finance and land management.

The British Horse Society is a source of advice for its members. It publishes many specialist leaflets on common problems and offers good local contact and hence local specialist knowledge. Similarly, the Association of British Riding Schools offers help to those going into that area. The National Pony Society, the National Light Horse Breeding Society (HIS) and the Thoroughbred Breeders' Association are all able to assist those contemplating setting up stud farms. Horses are now within the scope of the Rural Development Agency (formerly CoSIRA). This body is an excellent source of advice and guidance on financial matters, grants available, training possibilities and marketing.

Finally, when considering suitability, the check list should include:

- pleasing locality;
- access to main services;
- free draining land;
- a southerly aspect;

- good safe hacking;
- tolerant neighbours.

Layout and principles

To some extent existing buildings dictate the overall layout, but they do not necessarily control it. The need may be for good lateral thinking. An existing building which at first sight appears crucial to the layout of the new buildings may in fact be better off demolished! The gap so created opens up a range of possibilities. When designing the layout is the time to be brave and resolute and look to the future. Those working in the yard later may condemn the lack of vision or the expediency which resulted in a poorly sited tack room. Good layout is a good investment in equine, human and financial terms.

There are no tested standard plans as there are in some areas of agriculture such as the layout of milking parlours and of yards leading to the cow cubicles and silage area. There are four criteria to bear in mind:

- Is it right for the horses?
- Is it right for those who work there?

Fig. 2.3 Stabling, indoor school and accommodation built early this century to a standard which would now be prohibitively expensive.

Fig. 2.4 Stabling in an 'American Barn' system.

Fig. 2.5 Old cart sheds simply converted to make excellent stables.

Fig. 2.6 Young horses winter well in barns.

- Is it aesthetically pleasing?
- Is it safe?

In balancing these criteria, the horses must come first. The range of possibilities is greater than at first appears. The housing for horses round the world shows a wide variation within the good results group. It is erroneous to attribute a human outlook to animals and hence it is a mistake to say 'Well, how would you like to live in a ...?'

Horses have a different attitude to their environment than do human beings. They need plenty of fresh air and that is certainly missing from many stables. Bad stables have low roofs, no high outlet for stale air, poor air circulation and in some cases they even lack an inlet for fresh air. Horses need personal space in which to live without threat from a neighbour. This does not mean that stalls are necessarily bad, but it does mean that loose boxes with feed mangers facing each other through bars are bad.

Horses also need a regular and peaceful environment free from tension. This may be found in an old stone-built yard with doves, but it may equally be provided in a modern yard with pop music! Peace is disturbed by grooms who are tense or cross, irregular routines, sudden noises and events which are out of the ordinary. It is also disturbed by visitors who want to stroke the horses. Horses also need comfortable bedding, adequate food and water and regular exercise. This last feature is of particular importance in overall design which may include horse walkers, maneges, indoor schools and exercise yards. All these things take up large areas of space and are thus key features in designing the lay-out.

Consideration for the people who will work in the yard and care for the horses is also essential when planning the lay-out. 'Work study' is the examination of ways of finding the best and most efficient method of doing a job, especially in terms of time and effort. In our context, it is especially concerned with the route taken during the daily routines – morning and evening stables, tacking up and other regular tasks. Good layout can shorten the route and thus save time, effort and expense. Sometimes putting in a door or relocating the muck heap can make a great deal of difference to the daily life of a groom. Good design reduces drudgery and increases effectiveness.

Major decisions about the style of housing should be strongly influenced by employee considerations. One of the main reasons for stabling horses in barns is that it is quicker and easier for the grooms as well as being tidier than a row of loose boxes. The same argument applies to the use of stalls. Mares in stalls provide the speediest way of mucking out a large number of horses. A good drain will already have coped with the urine, the faeces are conveniently placed to load into the barrow and the bedding stays dry and needs little attention. Geldings are less helpful; they wet their bedding.

All stabling should look good and be appropriate to its function and to the site. Architects are often criticised for creating new designs which look out of place against existing buildings. In some cases, the criticism is well-founded; in others, the real criticism was that the offence was caused by the new building being 'different', and in retrospect has in fact blended in quite well. Colours, shapes, texture of materials, the outline from different viewpoints, and first impressions are all important considerations. In many cases, the additional cost may prevent one from using the more expensive materials; the good use of colour and careful landscaping can make cheaper materials quite as acceptable.

Moving earth to level sites so as to make banks can provide screens, and planned planting of trees, shrubs and creepers at the building stage can rapidly make a great improvement to the visual appearance of the premises. In the same way, good use of colour and choice of materials can vastly improve the interior of a building without any great increase in the overall cost. Design is the function of architects whose education prepares them to assist clients at all stages of the design and construction process, but the architect's client must provide adequate information on the site, project and budget, and fully understand and approve the architect's proposals at each stage. The client must be able to brief the architect adequately if he is to perform his professional functions properly. Both employees and clients will appreciate a stable block built with thought for its layout and aesthetic appearance.

Safety is the fourth criterion in layout. It is a major factor because of one's legal and moral responsibilities towards employees and members of the public. Safety is very important in riding schools or any other premises to which the public has access. In a riding school, for example, the design should provide for visitors to get directly to a reception or waiting area, thus avoiding the risk of their poking around the yard, upsetting the horses and causing an accident. In a stud, the layout will concentrate on the stallions which tend to be more peaceful if mares are not led past their boxes. Someone could be grooming a stallion when an in-season mare is led past and both groom and the mare's handler would then be put at risk. Good design takes such things into account. Figure 2.7 shows how a fire travelling with the prevailing wind moves away from the area of greatest danger and is an example of good design. Some horses are very protective of their feed to an extent which makes them difficult at feed time, especially if they have not been taught good stable manners.

Design to cope with Fire

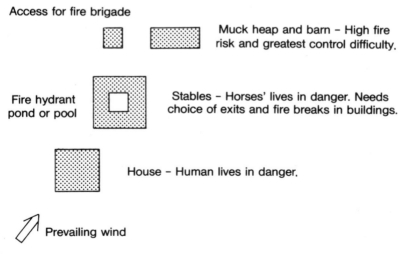

Access for fire brigade

Muck heap and barn – High fire risk and greatest control difficulty.

Fire hydrant pond or pool

Stables – Horses' lives in danger. Needs choice of exits and fire breaks in buildings.

House – Human lives in danger.

Prevailing wind

Fig. 2.7 Areas of greatest risk: downwind. Areas of greatest danger: upwind. This design also keeps the 'dust' from the barns away from the stables, thus aiding horse health.

Feed mangers in the far corner of stables are not only a waste of time; they also can create tension between horse and groom, and where there is tension there is danger. Mangers filled from outside are both quicker and safer.

Small, placid ponies do well in covered straw yards. Bigger horses and cobs prosper in stalls, but need daily exercise. Horses which include a stand-in day (when they are not exercised) as part of the weekly routine need to be in loose boxes. (Stand-in days only benefit employees; horses do better without them.) Thoroughbred mares have been wintered successfully in stalls when exercised daily on a horse-walker. Tense and highly-strung horses do better in loose boxes, which can be in barns or set around a yard. The cost difference between the two arrangements is less than the cost difference within each system.

The many items to include in a complete stable yard are shown in Table 2.1.

Table 2.1 Requirements of a stable yard.

(1) Loose boxes	(17) Locker and changing room
(2) Stalls	(possibly with shower)
(3) Stock yards	(18) Staff lounge
(4) Feed room	(19) Store – for paint, lawnmower,
(5) Hay store	etc.
(6) Straw or bedding store	(20) Garages and parking areas
(7) Bulk or back-up feed store	horsebox, tractor, staff, visitors
(8) Wash area: buckets, rugs, etc.	(21) Wheelbarrow park
(9) Wash area: horses	(22) Fire and security control
(10) Drying room	points
(11) Dirty tack cleaning area	(23) Clock
(12) Clean tack store	(24) Isolation box
(13) Utility box (clipping, heat	(25) Specialist stud units, e.g. stallion
lamp)	quarters, foaling unit, covering
(14) Manure bunker	and teasing yard
(15) Office	(26) Forge
(16) Lavatory	(27) Mounting block

Detail design

The guiding principles of detail design are that the end result should be safe, functional and labour-saving. For example, a manger on a tilt, swivel or hinge system or with a trap door of sufficient size to take a bucket above it is a simple essential if employees are to be well-paid and cost-effective. Similarly, the hay rack should be filled from outside; this not only saves time but allows for the rack to be lower in the stable and to be fitted with a mesh lid to prevent the horse lifting the hay out of the top. The lower fitting is better for the horse because it is less likely to get a grass seed in its eye; it is also better for the person whose job it is to fill the hay racks.

Automatic drinkers are another time-saving essential. Such devices have an unjustifiably bad reputation but most problems can be solved by installing them correctly. The supply tank should be fitted in the roof so that the system is gravity-fed rather than fed direct from the mains. The supply line should be fitted with a tap to each drinker, thus enabling ease of adjustment and maintenance. A drain cock must be fitted at the lowest point so that during very cold weather the system can be drained off each evening to avoid overnight freezing. There must also be a well-insulated tap for use during very cold periods. This water tap is best sited in the feed room, preferably over a big Belfast-style sink set near to the floor. The sink unit serves for washing buckets in an ordinary routine. Each stable needs a tie ring near the hay rack and another well away from it. Each tie ring should be fitted with a loop of parcel string or strong garter elastic (*not* plastic bale twine) so as to provide a weakest link to break if there is a fracas, so avoiding a broken head collar or the tie ring being pulled from the wall. When training horses to be tied up, a long line running through a strong ring or around a post or tree enables them to be properly handled.

It is pleasant for stables to face south, and the use of south-facing hatches allows for this: (see Fig. 2.8, which shows an economical stable yard). In this yard, the horses all face south but are tended from a central open driveway. Labour is thus reduced to a minimum under a traditional system of management.

Location of both tack and feed rooms is important as they are central to stable routines. The siting of the barn and muck heap are also critical. There is a possible advantage in siting the muck heap down-hill, if the yard is on a slope, since an empty barrow is easier to push up an incline. If muck is to be put into a skip or trailer for removal from the site, a sloping non-slip ramp will be required. The ramp should be sited so as to take advantage of any gradient and this could be a key factor in overall layout.

The major problem of feed rooms is that of rodents. Feed should be stored in metal bins. Sacks should be stored on low benching erected so as to allow for it to be swept under. A high degree of cleanliness and

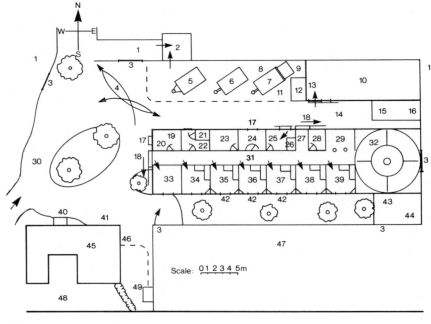

Key
1. Field
2. Field shelter/sick box
3. Gate
4. Lorry manoevring area
5. Caravan
6. Lorry or horse trailer
7. Trailer parked
8. Shavings
9. Platform
10. Barn for hay and shavings
11. Barrows
12. Ramp up
13. Tools
14. Delivery road
15. Tractor shed
16. Lean to
17. Window
18. Sliding doors
19. Telephone
20. Office
21. WC
22. Changing
23. Tack room
24. Wash room
25. Feed room
26. Fire point

27. Exit
28. Dry room
29. Electric grooming bay
30. Drive
31. Passage for box access
    (N.B. hay and feed without
    entering stable)
32. Horse walker with roof
33. Wash and utility box
34. Box 1
35. Box 2
36. Box 3
37. Box 4
38. Box 5
39. Box 6
40. Front door
41. Car parking
42. Open hatchways, horses'
    iookout
43. Lean to
44. Dump store
45. House
46. Back door
47. Manege 20 m × 60 m
48. Garden
49. Box gallery

Fig. 2.8 Example of a stable yard for six horses.

1. Select, pleasing locality, good site, tolerant neighbours, access to services, free draining land and southerly aspect.

2. Access to training facilities to complement manege etc. In particular – good safe hacking.

3. Aesthetically pleasing (looks good and appropriate to site and function) e.g. tiled roof towards house.

Section

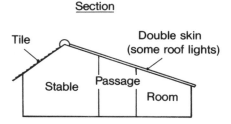

4. Labour-saving layout (see plan).

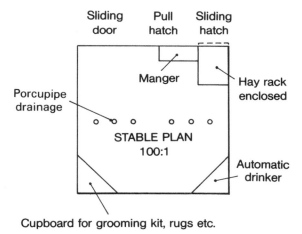

Cupboard for grooming kit, rugs etc.

5. Labour-saving features particularly to help with routine stable duties, i.e. feeding hay and concentrates, watering, grooming, mucking out.

6. Design for safety and freedom from accidents.

7. Provide for fire fighting and emergency evacuation, e.g. hose reel in building handy to barn. Telephone. Two exits. Also, prevailing wind blows from house to stable to barn.

8. Design to minimise disease, e.g. low dust (hay barn down wind), good ventilation. Sick box.

9. Easy to clean and low maintenance.

10. Privacy for house occupants when off-duty.

Fig. 2.8 Continued. Features of the stable yard.

hygiene is essential: spilt food is best retrieved from difficult corners with a heavy-duty vacuum cleaner. Food is moved fastest with a round scoop, but there should be a set of trial scales so that a check can be kept on the weight of a scoop of different ingredients. If there is a barley or linseed boiler it should be sited beside a window to allow for the escape of steam.

There should be two distinct areas in the tack room – one for cleaned tack and the other (or dirty area) for working in. The dirty area should be equipped with a sink and draining board, with a source of both hot and cold water. There must also be a high saddle horse for cleaning saddles as well as a bridle hook. Provision must be made for dirty tack awaiting cleaning. The clean area should catch the eye when entering the room; there must be space for bandages, rugs, head collars, whips, lunge gear, etc. Metal trunks are rodent-proof and if set on strong board shelves provide neat storage for rugs out of season. The tack room should have a low-heat source to warm the air sufficiently to prevent condensation. The tack room should also have a source of heat for its human users; a minimum working temperature is a legal requirement. A fan heater will generally suffice, and a wall socket for a radio or cassette player will also be appreciated when tack is being cleaned.

Provision for fire is essential but expensive; the local Fire Authority will be glad to give advice on the equipment needed, numbers of extinguishers, and so on. They are the experts and the Fire Prevention Officer's advice should be followed. He will visit the premises on request and his experienced eye may well detect dangers which can be eliminated by simple re-arrangement. In very small establishments, buckets containing sand are a cheap and easy provision for dealing with fire. Water buckets will also be needed and the best buckets for this purpose are those with round bottoms which cannot be used for anything else. They are hung up by the water trough ready for use. However, there should always be one or more fire extinguishers. There are various types of fire extinguisher; those coloured green contain a gas which can be used to extinguish fires of all types and which is highly effective. Additionally, there should be a fire hose of sufficient length to reach all points on the premises. Fire hoses and other fire-fighting equipment should be checked or tested regularly; when testing a hose, it must be fully unwound before it operates at full force. Larger complexes will need a special fire hydrant point and additional equipment.

Doors might be locked when a fire breaks out, so a small axe should be available; strong bolt-cutters are needed in case a gate is padlocked or there is a stallion on a chain. Alarm systems can be simple or complicated: metal rotary fire gongs are not loud enough – an old school hand bell is far better. Larger establishments should have a small electric fire siren, and if it is likely there will be a large number of people around the premises, there should be several points from which the siren can be set off.

In selecting building materials, the need to maintain a pleasant climate within the stable is paramount. A roof with good thermal properties will reduce rapid temperature changes. The worst type of roof is a low south sloping one of galvanised iron; it results in excessive overheating on a pleasant summer's day and drips with condensation at night. A boarded roof covered with roofing felt works well and looks best if roofing felt tiles are used. Traditional tiles look well, but they need a strong supporting roof structure. Corrugated cement sheets – they no longer contain asbestos – are cheap but they need spraying on the underside with insulating material once they are set in place. Stables made of wood provide a pleasant environment for horses, but tend to get eaten. Ideally, they should have a smooth interior right up to the eaves, thus avoiding the problem. If only kicking boards are to be provided up to 1.2 m (4 ft) high, the area above the boards should be lined to stop the timber ribs being chewed.

The doorway is the second area of destruction. Ideally, every wooden stable door should be fitted with an anti-weave grid to reduce chewing of the doorway. Anti-weave grids can be supplied by most manufacturers at no extra cost in lieu of a top door. Some wooden stables have the window beside the door; it is far better to specify that the window be set in the opposite wall. This lets in more light if not under an underhang and the window will not be obscured by the top door, if fitted. The window should be an opening one, protected by bars or mesh on the inside. The best forms of window ventilation are the 'Sheringham system' or louvres as both direct cold air upwards so that it mixes with the warm air in the stable. The latter have the advantage of less intrusion into the stable and so are safer. Stables should have an opening in the ridge to allow warm stable air to escape.

Floors are a great problem. They should be non-slip, hard-wearing and should not strike cold; provision must be made for drainage. The cheapest floor is one of rammed chalk which works well on well-drained soils but needs maintenance. Porous tarmac laid on a bed of stones also works well, but drainage can be a problem. Drains within stables tend to harbour disease and are difficult to clear if blocked. The exception is a properly installed system of 'porcupipes' which provide a row of small holes across the floor. Concrete is the most commonly used flooring material and is sometimes laid without a drainage slope because bedding can absorb the urine. Generally, it is better laid with falls to a back corner outlet and so into an open drain channel. This is easy to keep clean and will not harbour vermin. Overall design unity, ease of work and personal preferences must all be taken into account.

Facilities

Labour must be used more effectively as it becomes more expensive. Most stables require that many hours be spent in steady work such as keeping stabled brood mares fit, getting horses up from grass, routine exercise of fit horses, and limbering-up or cooling off after schooling or other strenuous work. This is very labour-intensive, and much of the steady work can be done on the horse-walker. While four horses are exercising on the walker, their boxes can be mucked out. The early horse-walkers tended to pull the horse's head up unless side-reins were used. The popular modern designs allow the horse to be free in a moving pen between the inner and outer rails. If the horse-walker is outdoors, the walkway must receive particular care: sand and shavings over concrete seems to provide the best service.

Military stables used to include lunge rings and these are still provided in some racing yards. Indoor schools tend to be costly. Generally, lungeing can be done in an arena which also provides for riding. For working horses, an outdoor arena measuring 20 × 60 metres is ideal; a little extra width is helpful if it is proposed to put a show jumping course on it. A useful compromise is an outdoor arena or school together with a 20 metre square barn which allows for work in bad weather and is also useful for breaking.

The floor material of arenas is a controversial subject. Indoors, the traditional mixture is sand and wood shavings or sawdust, together with salt or fullers' earth to retain moisture, finds wide acceptance. Outdoors, water is the main problem. Good drainage is essential, and this means that the drains must be laid, covered with stones laid on a membrane so they do not sink into the soil and topped with a second membrane to prevent the stones coming upwards, and a topping of the chosen surface material. In essence, the process is to build upwards from ground level away from the water table. This is shown in Fig. 2.9. Sand is still favoured as a surface because it does not degrade, but it can ride deep. This problem can be solved by the choice of sand or adding in elements to provide a firmer footing. The weekly and hourly amount of maintenance required is a further consideration. (An excellent but inexpensive booklet

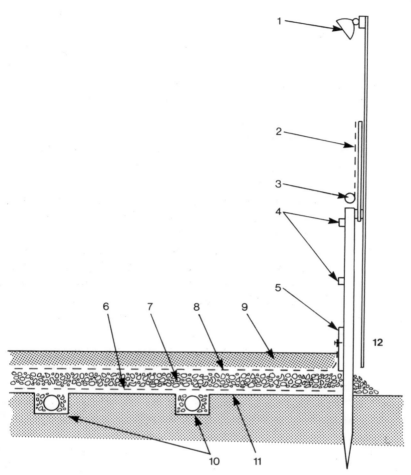

Key
 1. Lights as high as practicable
 2. Sight screen to 2.0 m where necessary
 3. Irrigation system
 4. At least 1.30 m high surround rails on inside of posts
 5. Treated timber edge boards
 6. Permeable membrane to stop stones sinking into the earth
 7. Layer of stone for firm base and drainage
 8. Second permeable membrane to stop stones rising
 9. Riding surface
10. Drains as necessary
11. Ground surface levelled
12. Riding surface must be above normal ground level to help drainage

Fig. 2.9 Construction of an outdoor arena. (Surface: sand, wood or other products.)

on the construction of all-weather riding arenas is available from the British Horse Society.)

A cantering track can be made cheaply by having the top soil scooped off and backfilling the excavation with about 10 cm (4 in.) of sand. Drainage pipes may need to be fitted in low-lying spots. Such a track will not be 'all weather', nor will it be as good as a racing gallop, but a 2 furlong (400 m) track is very useful in terms of faster fitness. Cross country fences need not be big for training; they should provide a variety of possibilities and are best set out like a show jumping course. The fences will be best if take-offs and landings are kept topped up with sand so that they do not get deep in wet weather.

When an indoor school is to be built, its basic design will be similar to an agricultural barn with outward sloping kicking boards rising to a height of at least 1.35 m (4' 6") sloping outwards at 10°. A height of 4.3 m (14 ft) to the eaves is adequate. Wide doors are required both for deliveries and maintenance. Lighting is by clear panels for daytime, with strip lighting for evening use. (A booklet on lighting sports areas is available from CIBS, Delta House, 222 Balham High Road, London SW12 9B5.) There should be a viewing gallery, however small; it may normally only house the trainer or instructor, but should always allow for other spectators. The gallery should be well insulated and efficiently heated; indoor schools can be very cold places. A layout for an indoor arena is shown in Fig. 2.10.

Under the Fire Safety and Safety of Places of Sport Act 1987 there are measures to enforce safety standards at indoor sporting events for spectators. A licence will be needed where the sports entertainment is the principal purpose for which the premises are being used. Thus every riding school which intends putting on shows and has a public gallery should have a licence. Certainly a licence would be needed if the public were to be charged for admission or were present in large numbers. Local authority safety experts will have to inspect the premises before a licence can be obtained.

Unless a side gallery is within the span of the building the uprights (stanchions) would obscure the spectators' view, so an end gallery may be preferred.

Accommodation

Accommodation for staff is often overlooked. In small establishments staff may live *en famille*, but a bigger enterprise may require purpose-built

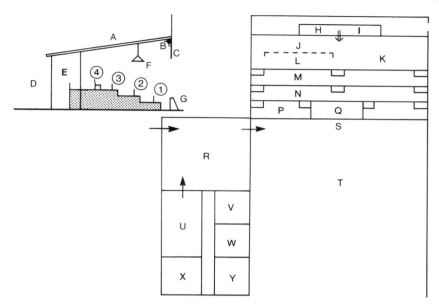

Key

A. Double skin roof
B. Loudspeaker
C. Heat retaining board
D. Section through the gallery
E. Passage
F. Halogen radiant heat lamp
G. Arena
H. Ramp
I. Steps
J. Standing
K. Gallery, space for wheelchairs
L. Row four

M. Row three
N. Row two
P. Row One
Q. Box
R. Covered collecting area
S. VIPs or dressage judge
T. Arena
U. Jump store
V. Competitors' viewing
W. Show office
X. Workshop
Y. Judges' box (show jumping)

Fig. 2.10 Layout of an indoor arena suitable for local shows.

or converted accommodation. All too often this is scruffy and well-nigh uninhabitable. Good staff deserve good working and living conditions. In some cases, provision must be made for accommodating clients as well. All accommodation should be adequate and of a high standard.

Essential requirements are a large boot park and area for wet-weather clothing – near to the back door. Drying areas for wet clothing are a must. Showers may suffice but hair dryers need plugs! Individual rooms are needed for all, except young clients who enjoy dormitory accommodation. Rooms must be able to cope with riding boots and other equipment, including the occasional saddle. Wholesome food and plenty of it is also essential. In self-catering establishments the microwave oven has done wonders for the communal kitchen. (Any form of catering facility however, must comply with the Food and Hygiene Act.) Caring for horses may not be highly remunerated and may entail long hours; it certainly deserves comfortable surroundings, warm and dry accommodation with adequate facilities and good food. There is no doubt that staff and clients who are disgruntled by their living conditions will create an unpleasant atmosphere and everyone will suffer.

3 Staff

Introduction

A competent and happy staff is crucial to the success of any business operation. The greatest care is needed in the recruitment and training of staff and all employees deserve a career structure which is in line with other industries. Satisfactory pay and conditions and a happy working atmosphere and environment are essential if people are to give of their best. Each member of staff is an essential link in the chain. Wise employers help their employees to appreciate that they are part of a team and the most important people in the industry.

Recruitment

Losing a member of staff does not necessarily mean his immediate replacement by someone with similar skills. A job vacancy gives the employer an opportunity to review the position and to appraise the overall staff situation. It is the right moment to consider the total skills of the whole work force as well as the present and future needs of the business. In some cases, of course, a person with identical skills may be essential – though no two people are alike in personal attributes. In most cases, though, the employer should consider not only the skills that have been lost because an employee has moved on, but also the skills which will be needed in the future. This is as important in a small establishment as it is in a larger one. The key lies in finding the right person for the particular job. The terms and conditions of the job are also important. Working with horses may be a vocation, but 'job satisfaction' cannot compensate for meagre rewards!

Job specification

It is essential to have a job specification. Before advertising for a new recruit, the employer should write out a full description of the job and what it entails, along with the characteristics of the ideal candidate. These will range through training, qualifications and experience, to personal qualities and attitudes. It may well be that the 'ideal candidate' does not exist, and so it is necessary to list the various characteristics sought as either 'essential' or 'desirable'.

Adaptability is an important asset in the horse industry: some people can learn new skills very quickly, but all horse staff must be adaptable. A candidate may lack a required skill and yet be so good in all other respects as rapidly to become a key member of the team. Training and education can provide the required skill and knowledge. They have an essential part to play at all staffing levels. Staff selection and training are inter-related. An existing employee may deserve promotion and yet need more training in a skill essential to the job. In such a case it may be worth deferring the appointment until the person is ready.

Listing the desirable characteristics of a proposed employee is not difficult. A checklist might be:

- *Age and physical factors*

Minimum and maximum ages. Health. Physique. Bearing. Speech. First impressions – these are of importance in a receptionist, for example. Ability to cope with pressure and stress is something not to be overlooked.

- *Attainments*

Education – general and special. Qualifications and experience. Past training. Training potential. Special knowledge and skills.

- *Aptitudes and interests*

Good with figures? Likes problem horses? Development and implementation of new ideas

- *Disposition*

Suitable for the job? Gregarious or solitary personality? Own initiative or routine?

- *Background*

Personal lifestyle and habits? (Family commitments can affect holidays and overtime.) Religious observances? Such restrictions are acceptable but should be known at the outset. The horse industry is demanding of people's time. If accommodation is offered, how will the applicant adjust away from home?

- *Career plans*

How the applicant sees the job is important. A career structure is important to those who wish to train to work with horses. His ambitions and potential must be considered. What are the job prospects? Promises that cannot be met should not be made.

Once the 'ideal candidate' is identified on paper, the vacancy can be advertised. Advertising may be internal, in local newspapers, and in the national equestrian press. Job vacancies should also be notified to the Department of Employment and to students through the various County Colleges of Agriculture with equestrian departments.

Drafting advertisements is an art. The advertisement should outline the job, make it appear attractive, and invite those interested to send for further details, whether by letter or telephone. The employer should prepare an information sheet which includes a detailed job specification and sets out the wages and other conditions, such as accommodation, keep of own horse, time off, transport, etc. This sheet should be sent to each enquirer. Telephone inquiries should be answered immediately: the pre-prepared information sheet can be slipped straight into an envelope and put in the post. In larger establishments, an application form may be desirable; in every case applicants should be asked to produce a brief career outline or curriculum vitae and a letter of application. This should set out a personal resumé as well as the applicant's qualifications and experience. It should also say why the applicant is looking for a new job and when he will be available. Employers should ask for one or two referees who can vouch for the candidate's character, abilities and experience.

Once the information is to hand, a preliminary selection can be made. Filling any job vacancy should be regarded as an important task. If there are few applicants it may be best to see them all on an informal basis until the appointment is made. Many positions are filled successfully in this way.

More senior jobs may attract many potentially suitable applicants and more formal procedures are needed. A short-list of six or so people should be made, and a day set aside for the interviews. Candidates should be invited for the morning which can be spent showing them round the premises, introducing them to other staff (if any) and chatting informally, answering questions as they arise. Lunch may be taken buffet-style, and formal interviews follow. Often by the end of lunch the interviewer has a fair idea of who the best candidate is – assuming that he still shows interest in the job! But the interviewer should keep an open mind; first impressions are not necessarily the best ones.

Interviewing

Interviews are of many types, but job selection, annual appraisal and disciplinary interviews are the most important. Everyone in business needs to grasp the basic techniques, most of which are common to all interviews. Both interviewer and interviewee must be properly prepared, and this is one reason why preparation of an adequate job specification is so important. The person conducting the interview must have studied the relevant information in advance.

Interviews should be planned, but a large desk and very formal setting are not necessarily advantageous. An annual appraisal interview for each member of staff is ideally informal as its purpose is to discuss the individual's progress, job perceptions and career development. Comfortable chairs and informality will be the order of the day. Disciplinary interviews warrant different considerations and should be more formal.

Selection interviews require special techniques as both parties need to get to know one another. The first few minutes should be spent putting the interviewee at ease and adjusting lines of communication. Rapport must be established. Someone who is tense may have difficulty in marshalling their thoughts and not say what they intended to say. The interviewee should be told the proposed format for the interview and be encouraged to ask questions.

At a selection interview the following points should be covered:

- The duties of the job.
- Duration of employment. Is the appointment a permanent one or is it seasonal or temporary?
- The working hours and time-off.
- The wage offered and how it is paid – weekly or monthly and whether in cash or by cheque.
- Overtime. Hourly rate of pay or whether time-off in lieu is given. Extra payments for work away from base, e.g. a groom travelling with a horse to a show, should be settled.
- Other conditions. Board and lodging, keep of own horse, use of car, entry in competitions, etc. If the post is residential, the standard of accommodation offered should be discussed, the interviewee having already seen it.
- The person to whom the employee is responsible and what other staff are to be his superiors.

Skilled interviewers use questions as a means of going forward and always remain in control of the situation. Questions asked should not prompt 'yes' or 'no' answers. Rudyard Kipling's words give the clue to the correct approach:

'I keep six honest serving men,
    They've taught me all I know.

Their names are "What" and "Why" and "When",
    And "How" and "Where" and "Who".'

Kipling-type questions invite the person being interviewed to open out. Other good lines of approach are:

'Tell me about ...'
'Yes, go on.'
'Why do you say that?'
'Do you prefer ...?'
'So you feel upset about ... Why?'
'So what you are saying is ...?'

In this way, the interviewer listens and understands; from time to time he checks to see that what has been said is correctly understood. Some answers at interviews are too long and wordy – whether because of nervousness or verbosity. A firm 'Right, thank you' may help to stop the flow and take matters on to the next point.

Once the candidates have been interviewed, and providing references have already been taken up, a decision can be made. In the horse industry, it is seldom necessary to delay making an appointment. The selected candidate should be invited back to the interview room and offered the job. Once the offer has been accepted, the disappointed applicants can be thanked and sent on their way.

Notes are a useful aid to concentration during any interview but can be overdone. Only outline notes need be taken during a selection interview. The position is different at a disciplinary or annual appraisal interview. In those cases, careful notes should be made and put on record for future reference.

Employment and employing staff

Whether someone working on the premises is an employee in the legal sense is not an academic question. Employees are those who have entered into or who work under a contract of employment. (Contracts of employment are discussed in Chapter 5.) It is a legal requirement that workers working 16 hours or more per week are given a written statement of the terms of their employment within 13 weeks from starting work. They must also be covered by employers' liability insurance in case they are injured or contract certain diseases whilst carrying out their job. Employees also fall in scope of the national health insurance scheme. Casual helpers – such as the schoolgirl who lends a hand at weekends –

are not usually classified as employees. However, if such a volunteer is kicked, she may be entitled to claim compensation from the business if the injury resulted from negligence. It is not possible to contract out of liability for negligence which results in death or personal injury, even if an indemnity has been signed by the the casual helper and his parents. This is a result of the Unfair Contract Terms Act 1977, of which s. 2 (1) provides that it is not possible to exclude or restrict liability in negligence for personal injury or death 'by reference to any contract term or to a notice given to persons generally or to particular persons".

Employees tend to take their example from the person immediately above them. A cheerful and hard working Head Lad or Head Girl with high standards normally means that there is an excellent atmosphere in the yard. Even a person of that calibre will get depressed if the employer is morose, weighed down with problems or acts irrationally. Employers should always be fair, predictable and reasonable. The atmosphere in the yard is important for the horses as well; human feelings and tensions communicate themselves to horses. If the horses are relaxed and happy they can use their energies to best advantage; sullen horses do not thrive or perform well.

Staff are usually the most expensive business cost and it is essential to the success of any business that staff have the right attitudes and skills. If one discounts the cost of the premises, labour costs usually amount to some 60 per cent of the total cost of keeping a horse. If this percentage is to be reduced, either the staff must be paid less – in which case they are probably of little use – or they should be able to look after more horses. This does not mean that staff should be overworked or that the horses' care should be skimped. It means that labour should be used more efficiently.

This requires labour-saving equipment as well as good routines. In some yards, the care of horses needs as much labour nowadays as it did centuries ago, but in almost every other area of activity progress has meant better and more efficient use of human resources. Only pack animals can be exercised as such, and only polo grooms can ride one horse while leading four others. Even they need assistance to get out of the yard, and the practice can be hazardous.

Traditionally, hunters were exercised on the basis of one being ridden and the other led, and in many cases still are. Today, horse-walkers, equine swimming pools and treadmills offer possibilities for exercise which requires less labour. Routine stable tasks also offer scope for greater efficiency.

In considering the employment of staff and the labour needed, the review should also include consideration of whether it is better to invest the money in a piece of equipment or another pair of hands. The matter should be costed carefully. Many of the more successful equine businesses are very well equipped, although it is debatable whether the good equipment has bred success or vice versa. Success certainly attracts high calibre staff and in this sense 'success breeds success.' Success in business often starts with the selection of the right staff.

Motivation

Most people are motivated to work by a mixture of pride and profit (Fig. 3.1). Pride is an innate human characteristic, just like the instincts of hunger and self-protection. It is pride which impels a homemaker to keep the house neat and tidy, and pride makes employees ambitious and successful.

In today's world, an individual's needs are greater because his expectations are higher. Advertising and the consumer society makes almost everyone feel that they 'need' items which were considered as

Fig. 3.1 People are like wheelbarrows – to make them go forward you must apply pressure to both handles – *pride* and *profit*.

luxuries only a generation ago. There is also the increased reliance on the use of credit facilities to buy things immediately rather than on saving for something specific. Financial benefits and rewards therefore loom large when someone is considering whether to take a job, although so-called 'fringe benefits' are also important, as discussed later.

The most valuable resource of any organisation is its human assets – the employees. The manager – the person in day to day charge – is the most crucial staff member. All too often the typical manager is merely average. A successful business needs a successful and well-motivated manager who is a leader, motivator, team builder, listener, good communicator and able to delegate successfully. The good manager always looks to the future and plans efficiently. He is not afraid to make decisions and has his priorities right. Good managers gain in self-confidence because they are trusted. In turn, they trust others and, having established good routines, leave others to put them into practice. In this way they have the time necessary to concentrate on those matters which call for their own expert judgement and decision.

The good employer will pay staff the best and most competitive rates he can afford. He will ensure that each member of his staff feels secure in the job, enjoys good living conditions and a satisfactory and pleasant working environment. He will also ensure that they work in such a way

---

The blasé manager's recipe for peace
1. Regard any new idea from the staff with suspicion – because it's new and because it's from below.
2. Insist that staff who want to use their initiative present their proposals in writing, in duplicate.
3. Ask staff to challenge and criticise each other's proposals (this saves the task of deciding – just pick any survivors).
4. Withhold praise and express criticism freely; this keeps staff on their toes and makes them feel vulnerable, so stops them getting too cocky.
5. Treat identification of problems as a sign of failure; this discourages people from letting you know when some areas are not going smoothly.
6. Keep total control and make sure that anything which can be counted is counted frequently.
7. Make decisions to reorganise or change policies in secret and then spring them on people unexpectedly – they may admire your decisiveness.
8. Ensure that any request for information is fully justified in writing – you don't want your business secrets falling into the wrong hands.
9. Delegate to the Head Lad, Head Girl or your Assistant responsibility for implementing any unpopular decisions you have made.
10. Above all else never forget that you already know all that you need to know about this business.

Fig. 3.2 The blasé manager's recipe for success (and stifling initiative).

that they are stretched and fulfilled. Most people respond well to trust, challenge and recognition as well as to financial reward. Staff should feel secure and part of the enterprise. They should be consulted and respected. Good work should be praised; less satisfactory work should be queried. Management mistakes should be honestly admitted. 'Please', 'thank you' and 'we' are words which are crucial for success. Some wit in industry produced 'rules' for stifling initiative: the rules in Fig. 3.2 are based on them.

Remuneration

Remuneration is a synonym for reward and is not merely proper wages. It includes all the benefits attached to a job such as board and lodging, keep of own horse, use of vehicle and so on. Accommodation provided for staff must be dry and warm in winter, and the cost of the necessary heating is inevitably expensive. Some staff accommodation in the industry uses metered heating for which the employees are expected to pay on an 'as used' basis. In some cases meters are unfairly and improperly set so that the staff pay over and above the true cost.

It may be practicable and in some cases essential to provide meals for staff. Where young staff are employed and provided with accommodation, nutritious and regular meals are essential.

If staff are allowed to keep their own horses, the costing is more complicated. There is the cost of keeping the horse, the loss of potential profit on another horse that might have been stabled and the cost of the time the employee spends in looking after the horse. Another perquisite may be the use of a vehicle in free time. Free use of a washing machine may be another benefit.

Training is often part of the package in the non-thoroughbred world especially where someone is progressing through examinations. Agreements ought to be set down in writing so that both parties can see the total value of the package and assess its implications.

Staff training

Staff development is an important aspect of management. It takes two forms:

- In-house training, which utilises the skills within the business to train staff.

- External or agency training. This may take a variety of forms – day release courses, short courses, study days, attendance at conferences and so on.

Training is recognised as a sound investment today, and there should be a clear agreement as to the training programme. Young staff will often be ambitious to progress to jobs of greater responsibility which demand new skills. If they are provided with adequate training they will be content and not anxious to move on quickly. The various factors affecting the acquisition of a skill are set out in Table 3.1.

Table 3.1 Factors affecting skill acquisition.

External	Teacher	Student
Environment	Enthusiasm	Physical ability
Facilities	Empathy	Age
Distractions	Skill at subject	Sex
Time Available	Skill as teacher	Maturity
	Skill as motivator	Intelligence
		State of mind
		Motivation
		Enthusiasm
		Time
		Money
		Preconceptions
	Duration and frequency of practice	

Skill has been described as competence built on knowledge and understanding. Attainment of skill in this wider sense is not just the capacity to perform a particular task, nor is it the empty acquisition of factual knowledge. It is the coming together of competence, knowledge and understanding and as such it is a proper goal for both educators and trainers.

Because, to make the best progress, it is necessary to gain both education and training, many school leavers intent on a horse career plan to go to college. Many of the specialist college horse courses are eligible for discretionary grant aid.

There are many new and developing techniques which can be utilised cost-effectively for staff training. The use of them means that it is cheaper to train existing staff than to rely on outside consultants or advisers.

Fig. 3.3 College students have a wonderful opportunity to start their careers with the best of preparation.

Training needs are partly exposed by staff appraisal interviews, which should be held for each employee annually. The purpose of such appraisals is to discuss the persons's hopes, aspirations, progress and training needs. The training needs of new employees should be discussed and agreed at the initial selection interview. What is agreed then should form part of the terms of the contract of employment. Another set of needs can be identified by considering the objectives of the business and analysing the skills necessary to meet them. Checking the existing skills of the present staff will identify any new skills likely to be required.

Student-centred learning

There are fashions and in-terms in all branches of management; 'student-centred learning' is in this category but is a convenient shorthand for an important concept. The term emphasises that teaching is about students and not about teachers and that the correct criterion in training is the amount that is learned rather than what is taught. The name also describes the technique. Students learn by doing, feeling, experiencing and enquiring. 'I hear and I forget; I see and I remember; I do and, only then, I understand.'

Simulation exercises are important and just as senior managers attend expensive courses where they play 'management games' and then discuss and analyse their approach to fictional problems, simulation can be utilised in all areas. For example, the plaiting of manes and tails can be learnt first on model necks and docks using bale string instead of hair. Leadership skills can be tested using jump poles, oil drums and ropes to perform a specific task, such as crossing a river without getting a load wet – just as in military leadership practical tests.

Riding instruction can be given on the basis of the student-centred technique. For example, instead of instructing a pupil 'Raise your left hand', the instructor might say 'Look where your left hand is now and consider how the horse is going, then try your hand a little higher and a little lower and see if it makes an difference'. In this way, the students learn to cope on their own and become aware of the relationship between rider and horse.

Teaching using this technique may seem more difficult at first. For example, the old routine of riding in formation may be easier, but better learning and teaching results from a compromise. Junior and novice riders at a riding school might first ride in formation, but then be allowed to ride in open order to try out the newly-acquired skills.

The process of learning

A skill is ability in a task, especially one acquired by training. It is usually made up of several smaller skills. Thus, when driving a car, to change gear requires clutch and accelerator operation, followed by gear change and then clutch and accelerator adjustment in opposite sequence, all performed without looking. This skill can be broken down into separate parts: e.g. learning the position of each gear first by looking and changing gear, learning to dip the clutch and let it up again smoothly without changing gear. The same analysis can be applied to any skill acquired by training.

The sequence of teaching a skill is:

- The complete skill is demonstrated at normal speed in context.
- The complete skill is then demonstrated very slowly so that each part can be identified.
- Each component skill is demonstrated and analysed into exactly what is involved.
- The student learns each of the component parts.
- The student then puts them together into the complete skill.
- The skill is practised to achieve satisfactory speed, efficiency, fluency and competence.

Table 3.2 Enabling activities. Activities which ENABLE students to learn more about horses.

ACTIVE — The student does			PASSIVE — The student has done to him/her	
Solving	Using	Creating	Indirect[1]	Direct[2]
An objective test (test of facts)	The student will use his/her knowledge	Write an essay, paper, notes or a book.	Read a book, magazine, paper, map, wallchart or poster	A study or tour visit
Practical test of problem solving	Practical practice (common in riding schools)	Produce a project	Watch a film strip, film loop, slides	A demonstration
Experiment to solve a problem	Role play	Give a talk	Watch and listen to film, video, tape, slide, television	A led discussion
Knowledge test	Discussion groups	Make a model	Listen to radio, tape, record	Instructor answers questions
Comprehension test	Business games	Draw a picture, plan or diagram	Smell various odours	Dictated or copied notes
Application test	Practical competition	Take a photograph	Feel shape and texture of various objects	External reinforcement (by the instructor)
Practical examination of competence	Practical examination of competence	Make a film, video, tape, slides	Visit show; study trade stands	External motivation (by the instructor)
Buzz group (impromptu discussion on a specific topic)	Teaching machines audio and/or visual	Act	Visit sales competition, display demonstration, exhibition	A lecture
Judge a competition	Programmed learning	Write a short story that is well researched	Study hand outs, selected passages from books and other publications and papers	
Place in order of merit	Fill in hand-out	Any form of synthesis where something is built up or put together.	Enter an environment which is an experience in itself e.g. The Spanish Riding School in Vienna	
Identification test	Use teaching pack		Be frightened by an experience	
Answer questions	Demonstrate skill		Enjoy an experience	
Literary search				
Evaluate information				

[1] May be instructor guided
[2] Instructor based activities

Students can learn because the instructor advises on every detail or by making their own mistakes. 'Feedback' is important in teaching, whether it is external – from the teacher – or intrinsic – from the student who recognises that the horse did not respond as required. Riding instructors who encourage intrinsic feedback develop riders with 'feel'.

Table 3.2 illustrates some activities which enable students to learn more about horses; not all of them are obvious.

Examinations

Good training requires 'markers' to show achievement; training for dressage enables both horse and rider to tackle more demanding tasks. For most skills, the 'markers' will be a series of graduated examinations or tests. The equestrian world is fortunate in that it has the National Levels (see Chapter 1) and the examinations of the various bodies are aligned with them. There are in fact over 70 examinations in the British horse world, and no employer can be aware of the significance of each one. Relating each examination to the levels helps understanding of the student's achievement and ability. The development of National Vocational Qualifications (NVQs) greatly helps promote a national system.

Continuous assessment is an important aspect of modern examinations. The system relies on the candidate's trainer to chart the individual's progress. In this way, each aspect of learning is checked rather than the small random sample of the tradition practical examination. It is sometimes alleged against this system that instructors will be biased in favour of their own trainees, but a moment's reflection shows that this is not so, since passing someone who is not 'up to standard' merely reflects on the instructor's reputation.

In practice, continuous assessment is well proven in other industries, and is often linked to a final traditional examination with an appropriate weighting. In some examinations series, external moderators are used to make random checks to ensure that the system has been fairly and properly applied. A moderator may interview each candidate briefly to ensure equality of treatment, and any borderline candidates may be tested in greater depth. The moderator then makes the final decision as to the pass/fail line. With experienced moderators, this system gives more accurate results than conventional examinations; it is also far more cost-effective! A similar system under National Vocational Qualifications allows approved Yard Managers to assess their trainees on the practical units of the examination and these results to be subject to random tests by verifiers.

Multiple-choice examination questions provide another accurate and cost-effective scheme. The entire syllabus can be swiftly checked; there are no personality or examination nerves problems, and misinterpretation of the questions is avoided.

Examining is an imperfect science, but it should at least be seen to be fair, reasonable, and produce knowledgeable graduates.

Table 3.3 Division of responsibilities between the head lad/girl and other staff.

Supervisor	Staff
Requirement	*Requirement*
A competent worker able not only to do the skills but also to teach, supervise and organise them. Able to assist and deputise for the manager.	A competent worker who is skilful and proficient within the range of routine tasks.
Qualities and abilities	*Qualities and abilities*
Confident, reliable, inspires confidence, gives orders without offence, maintains discipline and high standards, keeps accurate records, encourages and gives training to junior staff. Identifies with the aims and objectives of the establishment. Discreet and loyal. Safe. Leads by example.	Works safely with thought, care and efficiency to an agreed plan.
Typical tasks	*Typical tasks*
Work organisation.	Stable routines.
Horse care.	Basic horse handling.
Training and fitness to agreed plan.	Feeding and watering.
Care of facilities.	Routine health care.
Grassland practical management.	Riding to an agreed plan.
Linking records with office use.	Transporting.
Stud work to an agreed plan.	Keeping records.
Stable allocation	Grooming and stabled-horse care.
	Tractor driving tasks.
	Tack care.

Supervision

The key person in the team is the head lad, head girl, stud groom or supervisor; the title used is unimportant, but the person's role is vital. He or she is both team leader and taskmaster. The supervisor sets the standards required, whether of cheerfulness, time-keeping, loyalty, hard work, smartness, attention to detail or anything else. The team leader's personality must be buoyant so that morale can be maintained at difficult times. Different yards have different expectations of both supervisor and other staff, but a suggested division of responsibilities between supervisor and other staff members is shown in diagrammatic form in Table 3.3.

Giving instructions

The supervisor must give instructions concerning the work to be done, but an instruction without more is often insufficient. In many cases it is appropriate not only to tell people what has to be done, but also to show them how to do it. This is especially so with newcomers and it is important for the supervisor to explain why the job should be done in that way and in some cases why the job is necessary at all! The supervisor should emphasise the important aspects of the task, especially safety.

Routines

Routines are a regular method of procedure, and since much work with horses is unvarying it is important that staff establish and follow good routines. This important subject is discussed further in Chapter 7 where suggested timetables are given. One reason for good routine is that horses are creatures of habit; routine makes them feel happy and secure and so they thrive and perform better. Horses can also be dangerous, and all good routines require that tasks are done in the safest possible way, thus minimising or avoiding accidents. Many stable tasks are repetitive and following the agreed routine will be the most efficient way of doing the job. Effort is saved, productivity is increased, and high standards can be maintained.

The routine for keeping records, for example, ensures that accurate and up-to-date figures are available to provide management with the information needed to run the business efficiently. Good routine ensures that there is a daily programme, a place for everything and a check-list to ensure that all the chores are completed. In this way, the supervisor can

run an efficient yard which is a pleasure to work in with a minimum of
effort.

Safety

It is the responsibility of both employers and employees to ensure that
safe working conditions are observed. The Health and Safety at Work
Act 1974 imposes obligations upon both employers and employees to
take reasonable care both of themselves and others and people at work
must not be exposed to unnecessary risks to their health or safety.
Employers are obliged to provide a safe and healthy working environment: safe equipment, safe premises and safe systems of work.

The enforcement of the 1974 Act is in the hands of the Agricultural
Inspectorate who inspect equestrian premises and advise upon compliance with the legislation. It is impossible to make any working premises
absolutely safe and the employer's obligation is to ensure the health and
safety of employees 'so far as is reasonably practicable'. A basic duty is
also imposed upon all employees while at work, namely to act in the
course of their employment with reasonable care for the health and safety
of themselves, other workers and the general public, and to co-operate
with the employer and anyone else upon whom a statutory duty or
requirement is imposed, e.g. an agricultural inspector, to see that the
relevant statutory provisions are observed. The effect of all this is that at
any equine establishment all who work there, whether employees or
otherwise, together with visitors, all come under the Act.

Buildings and all work places must be safe in construction and properly
maintained. Safe equipment must be provided and properly maintained.
Veterinary products and disinfectants must be safely stored and used.
Gas bottles need special safe storage and appliances need professional
installation and proper maintenance.

Where five or more people are employed, s. 2(3) of the Act obliges the
employer

'To prepare and, as often as may be appropriate, to revise a written
statement of his general policy with respect to the health and safety at
work of his employees, and the organisation and arrangements for the
time being in force for carrying out that policy, and to bring the
statement and revision of it, to the notice of all his employees.'

Shorn of the legal verbiage, compliance with this requirement includes three elements: (a) a written safety policy, (b) organisation and (c) arrangements for carrying it out.

A written safety policy

The employer must prepare and issue a written policy statement outlining his safety and health philosophy. This must indicate the commitment of management and employees to the implementation of that policy. It need not be a lengthy document and the Health and Safety executive have published a booklet *Writing Your Health and Safety Policy Statement* which is available from HMSO (ISBN 0 118 83882 2) which gives guidance on preparing the statement and lays down the important points using page by page examples. The statement must cover the intent to comply with the statutory provisions and must lay particular emphasis on safe work routines and stress the importance of co-operation from the workforce and of good communications. It should be signed by the employer or a partner or senior director. The policy must be kept under review and the written statement amended when necessary.

Organisation

Even in a small business it is necessary to have a clearly drawn picture of the line and functional responsibilities of the people responsible for health and safety. If necessary the statement should define the responsibilities of named senior and junior members of staff both with regard to health and safety generally and to emergency situations. Those named must have adequate information and authority to perform their responsibilities.

Arrangements

The arrangements for carrying out the policy must be tabulated clearly, e.g. line responsibility for health and safety. Likely hazards must be identified and listed together with rules and practices for avoiding them. The arrangements for dealing with fire, injury and other emergencies must be spelled out. The arrangements for providing instruction, training and supervision must also be made clear.

All this is really common sense, and of course a written statement does not prevent accidents; the policy must be implemented. Table 3.4 sets out a typical safety code for an equine business; this should be distributed to all staff. It is not the written policy required by the Act – that has to be written by the management of each business, according to its needs.

Table 3.4 Typical Safety Code.

- Consideration of safety for people must override all others.

- Be mindful of the safety of persons, stock and equipment.

- Do not use faulty equipment – report it.

- Personal: Secure long hair, keep finger nails trimmed, keep jewellery to a safe minimum, wear suitable clothing and footwear for the work being done. Wear a hard hat to current BSI specifications, adequately secured at all times when mounting, dismounting and riding; also when breaking and assisting stallions at service. Wear gloves when there is a risk to hands through sudden pulls on lead ropes or lunge lines.

- Riding out: Only those with specific authority to do so may ride on the roads. Keep to the left. Keep led horses on the left of the handler. Avoid pavements and mown grass by houses. No smoking. After sunset, lights and reflective clothing must be worn whether riding or leading. Take care when passing pedestrians; particularly go slowly if passing them on bridleways. Show courtesy to other road users. Thank all drivers – whether they slow down or not. Abide by the BHS publication *Ride and Drive Safely*. Inform on route before departing the yard.

- Around the yard: Know and be able to apply the fire drill. No smoking except in the designated rest area. Horses to be tethered for mucking-out.

- Stud: Avoid leading mares or stallions past each other, especially during the stud season. Avoid scented soaps and perfumes when working with stallions.

A proper first aid kit must be provided and maintained in good order. Staff should be encouraged to seek immunisation against tetanus. An effective rodent control programme must be maintained. Staff must be provided with protective clothing where appropriate, e.g. hard hats, and advised on their correct fitting condition and use. Employees' attention should be drawn to matters of personal hygiene such as the need to wash hands before eating so as to guard against Weil's disease which is spread by vermin contamination.

Those working in dusty conditions or handling hay or bedding rife with fungal spores must be provided with respiratory protection equipment. Workers must be instructed in safe working procedures and there should be a planned programme of training which should include an induction programme for newcomers. The use of unsafe or makeshift equipment must not be condoned and there must be adequate supervision to see that safe working practices are taught and then observed. Damaged fingers result from failure to wear protective gloves, damaged toes from failing to wear protective boots, and damaged backs from faulty lifting techniques.

All new employees and trainees, for example, should be shown, trained and regularly checked to ensure that heavy loads (maximum 82 kgs/ 180 lbs) are handled, lifted and carried correctly. The main principles of safe lifting are shown below. Correct technique reduces the likelihood of

---

- *Assess the situation:*
  Dress – boots, gloves, etc.
  Equipment – pitch fork, bale hook, pulley, trolley, jack, lever, etc.
  Assistance – machine, team, mate, etc.
  Reconnoitre – safe object, safe route, safe landing zone, safe weight.

- *Stance:*
  Feet apart – balanced; one foot forward.
  As close as possible to the object.
  Back straight, chin in.
  Legs bent.

- *Grip (Lifting from floor):*
  Hand close and under weight or object clutched close to body.

- *Vision:*
  Do not block your view.

- *Lift:*
  Up and forwards – use leg muscles (calves, thighs, buttocks) but *not* back muscles.
  Do *not* twist or bend your spine.
  Keep weight close to body.

- *Carry:*
  Do not hurry, easy breathing, short steps.

- *Deposit:*
  Reverse of lift.

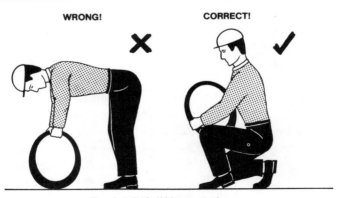

WRONG!   **CORRECT!**

Fig. 3.4 Safe lifting technique.

damage to back or rupture; it reduces fatigue and improves efficiency (see Fig. 3.4).

The Act requires there to be one 'sanitary convenience' (toilet) for up to five staff (including trainees and part-timers) and separate facilities for both sexes if there are more than five staff. These facilities must be private, under cover, properly lit and have properly fastening doors. The interior of separate sex toilet rooms should not be visible to members of the opposite sex and urinals must not be visible from any place where people work or pass (unlike the accepted style in France!). The facilities must be kept properly supplied. Flush toilets are obviously preferable but chemical or dry toilets are permitted. There must be at least one washbasin for up to fifteen workers and it must be conveniently accessible to the workforce and be kept in a clean and orderly condition.

HM Agricultural Inspectorate issues documentary guidance and some points of interest are:

- On studs, stallion handlers should generally be aged between 18 and 65.
- During covering at least three people should be present.
- At foaling, someone should not go into help a mare alone. Assistance should be summoned.
- The recommended maximum ratio of instructors to pupils in riding schools is:

Assistant instructor   1: 4
Intermediate instructor   1: 8
Instructor   1:10
On a hack, the suggested ratio should be one member of staff for each six riders.

These ratios may be varied for specific individuals after a careful management appraisal.

Discipline and Grievances

Every business except a small employer should have a formal disciplinary procedure so that the employee can be treated fairly and in accordance with natural justice if he steps out of line.

There should also be a grievance procedure so that employees know what to do if they are dissatisfied. Ideally, grievances should not reach a formal stage because good communications mean that the manager or supervisor has already spotted that something is amiss and initiated a discreet inquiry into the problem. The difficulty may be of a personal nature, and friendly counselling may be received and appreciated. The problem may arise from a misunderstanding or from a personality clash; again, once the cause is identified, a solution can be found. There should be a strong team concept in the business and the working team should be given the opportunity to ask questions and to discuss issues.

Discipline is a skill calling for sensitivity, courage and good judgement. A person who has done wrong will usually accept a fair reprimand and go back to work in reasonably good humour. Occasionally, it may be appropriate to be tolerant or turn a blind-eye, e.g. someone who had sat up all night with a sick horse would be justifiably aggrieved if, next day, they received more than a gentle reminder for a lapse in routine.

If an employee does fall seriously out of line, then a clear verbal warning should be issued. He or she must know the nature of the fault alleged against him, and be given a fair opportunity to state his case. The employee is entitled to appeal to a level of management not previously involved in the matter.

If a verbal warning is given, it should be recorded in the employee's file. A subsequent lapse may merit a further verbal warning, which should also be recorded. Termination of employment is a last resort, and its legal and practical implications are discussed in Chapter 5.

4 The office

Introduction

Every business enterprise needs an office where the inevitable clerical work can be done, records stored and visitors received. Office work is just as important as work in the yard, and good organisation can reduce the 'chores' aspect to a minimum. An office is essential to the efficient and profitable running of any business. In a small horse business, the office may well be a room in the house or even part of a room. Even in a home-based business, an effort should be made to provide separate accommodation from the family living-space. The principles of office organisation are identical whether the office is part of the working complex (as this chapter assumes) or a room in a house.

Organisation

Since offices are communication centres they should be strategically placed to intercept visitors, receive mail, store records which are available to the yard if needed, and keep in touch with staff. In practical terms this means that ideally the office should be sited by the entrance gate and clearly labelled as 'Office and Reception' so as to leave no doubt that visitors should call there.

If possible, there should be a separate reception area. There should be a bell connected to a yard or house bell and a notice stating that if the office is unmanned, the visitor should ring and wait. Dependent on the arrangement of the office, a buzzer can be useful even if the office is staffed full-time. Even if there is a full-time secretary, arrangements should be made for other members of the staff to undertake reception duties if he or she is absent. A notice outside the reception door should show the hours of attendance and give a telephone number for emergency contact. The notice can show other useful information such as the nearest pay telephone, the owner's address, etc.

Some riding schools undoubtedly lose business because of the poor first impression created by the reception area and office. If it is poorly decorated, furnished badly and is dirty and disorganised, customers may reasonably assume that the remainder of the establishment is equally shoddy. It is not necessary to spend a great deal of money in order to give the right impression but a neat and tidy layout and cleanliness must be the order of the day.

A stud farm or dealing yard must necessarily set similar first impressions. There must be a suitable area in which to make the bargain and deal with any necessary paperwork. A pound or two spent on refreshments for a customer in such cases will only be a tiny percentage of the overall transaction. The smaller business has neither the means to afford nor the need for a smart foyer with a receptionist and well-dressed sales-people eager to close a deal, but the horse world can learn from other areas where such things are justified. Certainly, the reception areas at some of the bigger studs warn potential customers that the prices are likely to be high. Some training yards have the rule that owners should visit by appointment only and this certainly makes sense. Where this rule applies, the yard has a drinks party for all owners once a month, thus establishing camaraderie between the owners who feel that they are members of a rather exclusive club. These trainers may well, on accountants' advice, be able to claim part of the costs of decorating and furnishing some rooms in their homes as a legitimate expense for tax purposes.

In many horse businesses the working office will be in the owner's house and the tack room will double as a reception area in the yard. Even here, attention should be paid to reception and office duties in the training of staff.

Office Routines

For equestrian businesses, office routines can be divided into six main areas:

- people;
- horses;
- finance;
- estate;
- marketing;
- competitions.

These subdivisions are very broad and not in any order of importance and the routines actually followed and records kept will depend on the nature of the enterprise.

People

Staff records must be maintained, not only to comply with legal requirements but for other purposes as well. There should be a personal file for each present and former employee and a general one for unsuccessful job applicants as well. Employees' personal files will include a copy of the written contract of employment, training programme, annual reviews, disciplinary notes, holidays and so on. PAYE and National Insurance records must also be maintained. Personal data kept in computerised form is now subject to control under the Data Protection Act 1987, which means that it must be made available to the individual on request as well as being securely guarded from intrusion. It also means that if personal records are kept on computer this fact should be notified and registered on a form from the Post Office. An Incident Book (formerly Accident Book) must be maintained in which any accidents can be recorded.

Horses

The records needed will depend on the nature of the enterprise; a stud will need different records from a riding school.There should be individual files for each horse giving purchase details, competition entries and performance, expenses, veterinary attention, farriery and any routine health treatment. Livery stables, studs and some other establishments need a monthly routine of invoicing and credit control. A useful system is to have separate books for Veterinary Routines and Farriery which can be completed at the time of the visit. Carbon duplicate books are useful because the top copy can then be inserted in the individual horse's file while the duplicates remain in the yard. There should also be Stock Books, Tack Books and possibly a Feed Book.

Finance

Accurate financial records are essential for legal, fiscal and control purposes. All expenses and income should be properly recorded in a form agreed with the accountant. Certain statutory PAYE and related records must be kept. General financial records should be prepared in a readily understandable way. Most equine business can use a single entry or Cash Analysis book, with the figures totalled monthly. In small businesses the record-keeper may well be the owner. In other cases, the secretary or person responsible for finance will be engaged on a part-time basis and use may be made of the local mobile farm secretarial service. However, even with professional help basic records must be kept on site – including a petty cash book. Any cash or other payments should be recorded as they come in and all cheques should be banked regularly. PAYE, income tax and National Health Insurance contributions are something not to be overlooked and VAT records must be maintained and supporting documentation readily available against a visit from HM Customs and Excise who are not noted for their kind-heartedness or willingness to overlook errors and omissions.

Estate

This term covers the management of the land and buildings and any equipment and machinery, together with any associated agricultural or other enterprises. Again, the records can be kept simple but are important.

Marketing

Marketing strategy, advertising, public relations, new ideas and develop-ments, and monitoring marketing activities all need proper attention in the office. It is all too easy to be so involved in caring for the horses and the general routines of running the business that this area becomes neglected.

Competition

Racing and competition stables need sound routines to cope with entries. In the racing world, not every entry made is followed up and this is an expensive feature of racing. Submitting entries may require the payment of subscriptions to various organisations, registration with a particular body and so on. Such matters all fall within this routine. Subscriptions to organisations should be paid as they fall due.

The keeping of records is a chore, especially when a conventional filing system is used. Staff will need strong motivation to keep records accurate and up-to-date. Only records which will be used should be kept; their usage will partly dictate the method of filing them. Records which are difficult in terms of access and retrieval mean that they will be used less and so are less worthwhile.

Equipment

The basic office equipment is a suitable desk and chair together with a filing cabinet. Second-hand office equipment is readily available, and little effort is required to produce a co-ordinated office image. Other essential equipment is a telephone and a typewriter (or word processor) and calculator (or a personal computer). The usual office supplies of notepaper, envelopes, carbon paper, paper clips and so on present no problem.

It may well be that most conventional office equipment is now obsolescent in light of the ready availability of relatively cheap personal computers, although the time of the 'paperless office' is far off, and conventional records must necessarily be maintained.

Personal computers

Whether or not to purchase a computer – and if so which one – is a difficult question for many people. In fact, even a small business will benefit substantially. The costs of buying a small computer have tumbled over the last few years so that the outlay will not be major. However, deciding to buy a computer is not a simple matter. There are various models and each of them have different features.

The simplest type is a dedicated word processor which replaces the typewriter. This speeds up letter-writing and makes the handling of correspondence easy. It will also produce standard letters which can be 'personalised'. A standard letter can thus be sent to each client looking as if it has been personally typed, since the word processor will insert the individual's name and address and personal opening and a reference to the addressee's horse by name into a standard format.

Dedicated word processors can be very sophisticated but few of them are as powerful as personal computers.

Those in the horse business are well advised to purchase a modern microcomputer since it will be more powerful and have more facilities than the word processing type, if only because with a suitable program the computer can be used to do the accounts. It is not necessary to know how computers work in order to use them, though unfortunately the computer industry has created a jungle of jargon which is intensely annoying to those outside the specialist field. Computers become an obsession with some people, almost a religion; they insist on putting everything on computer and spend many happy hours playing with them. Much computerised information can be recorded more simply on paper and filed and be retrieved just as rapidly.

Independent computer consultants can advise on an appropriate system, but they mostly concentrate on the more sophisticated needs of complex businesses. Apart from specialist computer shops, some of the major high street shops now have computer sections and advice is readily available. For most people ease of use is essential. If records are to be kept on computer the need is to be able to call them onto the screen with minimum of fuss, correct or up-date, print out if necessary, and then store.

A suitable computer system for those in the horse business is available as a complete package, including the necessary programs, for under £1000 at 1989 prices. The system consists of the central processing unit, the keyboard, a screen and a printer (hardware), together with word processing, management and financial programs (software). There are many accounting software packages available, some of them extremely complex. All that is needed is a program which will cover Revenue, Expenditure and Balance Sheet Accounts, and VAT (including the Cash Accounting Scheme). Most programs will cope with all normal routine transactions, including such essentials as bank reconciliations. Many calculations can be performed automatically – for example, balances against budget and totals for the current period against last year's totals for the same period. Other programs for the computer can handle stud records, riding school bookings and so on.

Reliability of the complete package and back-up service is important, and it is probably best to enter into a service agreement with the retailer. In fact, microcomputers are generally very reliable, and become more sophisticated every day.

Communications

The telephone is another vital piece of equipment, and a wide choice is available. A cordless telephone is extremely useful; it will operate around the yard and so can be answered even when riding! If, to answer an inquiry, it is necessary to consult someone else or look at the records, the conversation can be continued whilst looking for the person or file. Cordless telephones are inexpensive and easy to install. A telephone answering machine is essential for a business receiving impulse inquiries.

For example, the owner of a brood mare may decide to telephone the owners of possible stallions, and if the stallion owner is out will be able to leave a message. People are no longer so reluctant as they were to speak to a machine, and the initial cost is small. It is not worth hiring a telephone answering machine nowadays as such a small capital outlay is involved in purchasing one.

Stationery

Good quality paper and envelopes and a well-designed letter heading provide a business with a good public image. Every communication conveys the image of the business. The first essential is to choose a 'house style' in colour of paper, type of print and possibly a logo. A logo is the emblem or symbol by which the business is recognised. It should be simple and easily recognisable, and all of its potential uses should be considered before a choice is made.

Examples of logos include the yellow shell of the Shell Petroleum Company and the distinctive circled letters ICI of Imperial Chemical Industries plc. The business logo should indicate not merely that it is an equestrian business, but also that it is *the* particular business. Well-known examples of logos in the horse world are the cocked hat of Wellington Riding and the horse's head with a bear and ragged staff of Warwickshire College.

The cost of professional design and layout is relatively small, and a design service is offered by most of the national printing franchises as well as by many ordinary printers.

The chosen colour for the notepaper or the colour and style of type should be used on all printed matter. It can also be carried through on the stable doors and paintwork. It should certainly be used on the business notice-board at the entrance to the premises where the name and business logo can be proudly displayed.

Insurance

Every business needs insurance and it may be conveniently to find an insurance broker who will advise and arrange the cover which is needed. Insurance broking is now strictly controlled, but it is still up to the owner to decide on the extent of cover required and the 'best buys'. The National Farmers' Union offers a comprehensive service to its members and has local agents to give advice. A business affiliated to the British Horse

Society or another organisation will find that there are especially advantageous insurance arrangements arranged through the organisation's specialist brokers. Certain insurance is compulsory, e.g. under the Employers' Liability (Compulsory Insurance) Act 1969 which requires all employees to be covered for any injury they may suffer in the course of their employment and under the Riding Establishments Act 1964 for third party liability sustained while clients are riding or receiving instruction.

The many types of insurance may be put together in a comprehensive policy covering many eventualities – vehicles, employers' liability, public liability, personal insurance, horses and premises.

Vehicles

Third-party insurance cover for every motor vehicle using the public roads is mandatory. It covers damage to other vehicles and people when there is liability. More valuable vehicles are usually insured comprehensively so as to cover the cost of repair or replacement in case of an accident. In addition it may be sensible to take out membership of one of the national breakdown help and 'get you home' schemes: this is a form of insurance. If a vehicle carries 'goods' for 'hire or reward', it must be licensed either for 'farmers-goods' or as a haulier's vehicle. This is essential if, as is normal, livery clients are charged for transport to competitions or hunting. Infringement of the regulations or of the obligations involved in the licences is an offence and failure to comply with the terms of the licence may mean that the insurers are not liable.

Employers' liability

This is compulsory in respect of all employees in case they are injured or pick up certain ' diseases whilst carrying out their work. Working with horses is a high risk occupation. The amount of cover must be at least £2 million in respect of claims arising out of any one occurrence, but many policies give unlimited cover. The Employers' Liability Certificate must legally be displayed where the staff can see it, e.g. on the office wall. It is a criminal offence not to display the certificate.

Public liability

Any establishment open to the public should take out public liability insurance to cover potential liabilities to members of the public who may be injured. Riding establishments seeking a licence must establish that they are properly insured against liability for injuries sustained by riders and injured third parties. A stud having an open day or a school holding a gymkhana can take out suitable insurance to cover just that event.

Insurance policies of this type usually contain specific conditions which must be observed if the cover is not to be invalidated. (Any insurance policy received should be read with great care to find out exactly what is covered and also the particular terms and conditions.) A common requirement is that all riders must wear properly fitted hard hats to the current British Standard specification. In that case, a groom riding with the hat's chin strap unsecured might possibly be uninsured because modern hats must have a secured chin strap. Similarly, if a client is hired or loaned a hard hat, it must be of current BSI specification and correctly fitted and worn. An instructor should always check that this is the case and make the necessary adjustments.

Both the terms of insurance and the owner's legal liability under the law of negligence require that proprietors of equestrian businesses should warn the public of the potential risks involved with horses. It is no longer possible to exempt oneself from negligence liability resulting in death or personal injury, but in certain circumstances the law recognises that voluntary assumption of the risks involved may amount to a defence to an action for damage or injury brought against the person responsible.

It is therefore a sensible precaution to have suitable warning notices on the premises. One should state simply: 'All visitors should report to reception on arrival'. A second notice, in the reception area, should be along the following lines:

(1) Horses kick, bite and move quickly in certain circumstances so take proper care.
(2) Do not go near to the horses unless supervised by staff.
(3) All clients must read and follow our safety code.

The safety code should also be displayed.

By this means, clients and visitors are warned in advance, and there is thus less chance of someone getting injured. If someone were injured, then adequate warnings of these sort could well mitigate potential liability.

Personal insurance

Those who work for themselves should be adequately insured. They may need to employ someone else to do the work if they are ill, and they may require protection against loss of income. Various assurances of this type are available and any competent broker will be able to advise. A personal accident policy will pay a set amount each week for a stated period; other policies pay until normal retirement age. Additionally, the self-employed may need private health insurance tailored to their special needs. Private health insurance is not expensive and there are various types of policy. Most of them cover hospital accommodation charges, surgeons' and other fees and expenses, and some provide a cash benefit as well.

The self-employed should also consider taking out a personal pension policy and tax relief is available on the premiums. Some policies are linked to equity investments or unit trusts, but all of them offer an option on retirement of a fixed sum each month or of a lump sum and a reduced pension. They can also have provision for a surviving spouse. As the rules are changing constantly, the advice of an accountant should be obtained before a decision is made.

Many businesses operate partly on money borrowed from a bank or other financial institution, whether the borrowings are secured by a mortgage or not. It is often a condition of such loans that the borrower should take out a personal life insurance and the costs are variable. Some policies are initially expensive but reduce in cost as the term proceeds; others have a fixed rate throughout their duration. The choice is a matter of personal needs and bank managers and accountants are useful advisers.

Horses

Insuring a horse shares the risk of losing it. Insurance is available to cover accidents and injuries to or sickness and disease of horses and ponies as well as their loss by theft or straying. In some cases, the loss of a horse may be covered by a more general policy, e.g. in a building contents policy which may, dependent on its terms, cover against the loss of livestock through fire. It is a matter of commercial judgment as to whether horses are worth insuring specially as the cost can be quite high. Horses of exceptional merit may well be worth insuring and individual owners may wish to insure their horses both for loss and for loss of use. This last-named type of insurance costs more than the conventional policy, but if it is taken out the insurers will pay a percentage of its value if it becomes incapable of doing the specified activity. Policies may also cover such items as loss or theft of tack and veterinary expenses – usually as optional extras. An important consideration for all riders (whether in business or not) is to have cover against any accident involving a third party or parties. A runaway horse or one out of control can do a great deal of damage, and its owner could face a substantial claim if negligence is established.

Premises

As with domestic premises, business premises should be insured against the usual risks such as damage by fire, exceptional weather conditions and so on. Contents will need separate insurance. It is sensible to insure hay or straw in storage. Tack is expensive and is a high-risk item and should also be insured. Even if insured, loss of tack causes a great deal of inconvenience and so it is worth taking precautions to see that it is safe. Precautions may include a burglar alarm and other warning systems, and a useful free source of advice is the Crime Prevention Officer from the local police force.

Accounting procedures

Petty cash

Major items, such as a new saddle, should be paid by cheque against an invoice, thus providing a record of the transaction which will be entered in the cash analysis book. Smaller items, however, can be paid for in cash, and cash transactions must be strictly controlled. A sensible petty cash system is to have a 'float' of (say) £50 in a locking cash box, the money being drawn by cheque from the bank and 'petty cash' being entered on the cheque counterfoil. As cash payments are made, they are marked in a petty cash book which is kept with the box. Business expenses paid for in cash out of one's own pocket when away from the yard are also reimbursed from the same fund, and the relevant entry is made in the book. Receipts should always be obtained if possible. When the cash float is running low, it is topped up by way of cash from the bank, and the petty cash book and contents of the box should be reconciled.

An alternative method of petty cash control is to use the imprest system, whereby at the end of each month the float is made up by exactly the right amount so as to restore the opening figure.

Book-keeping: the cash analysis account

All business enterprises must keep an accurate record of all receipts and payments during the financial year. An accountant can advise on the appropriate system, but if the accounts are kept manually (and not on computer) a simple procedure is best. A well-tried system is based on the use of the single entry or cash analysis account book in which all receipts and payments of money are entered as received or made. The book is divided into columns so that items can be classified; receipts are entered on one page, and payments on another. The figures are totalled monthly and then can be reconciled with the bank statements. The headings of each column will depend on the nature of the enterprise, but a typical equine business might use:

Receipts
Livery fees
Instruction
Sale of horses
Transport charges
Sundries

Payments
Hay and straw
Concentrates
Transport costs
Insurances
Wages and National Insurance
Rates
Mortgage repayments
Bank charges and interest
Subscriptions

In both cases there should be columns for Value Added Tax (VAT).

One book is kept for each business year, and the loose-leaf form may be found most convenient. The book (or the pages for the year) are submitted to the accountant at the end of the year together with all supporting records – the petty cash book, wages book, receipts, invoices and the like so that the business accounts can be audited for submission to the Inland Revenue. The accountant will prepare the business's profit and loss account, which will include other items such as depreciation of equipment and, of course, the audit fee.

Using this system means that only two other books are essential: the petty cash book and a wages book. The wages book shows the details of each employee's weekly earnings, with columns for gross wages, nett wages, income tax deducted and the employee's share of National Insurance contributions. The weekly total of the gross wages is then transferred to the cash analysis book; income tax and National Insurance contributions (including the employer's share) will be sent by cheque to the Collector of Taxes in due course, and the employer's share of the National Insurance is also entered in the cash analysis book as a labour cost. This method involves the minimum of effort and the only other essential book-keeping records are the bank statements, cheque book counterfoils (properly filled in!) and stubs of the in-payment slips. Since the majority of banks no longer give itemised statements showing the person to whom payments have been made, it is wise to record the number of any cheque against the appropriate entry. If any payments are made by bank standing order these should not be forgotten.

All payments and receipts should go through the bank account, and thus the cash analysis book and bank statements will match up, provided that any bank charges are entered into the cash analysis book. The bank is the one trader who fails to send a bill! The money kept in the current account should be the minimum needed for trading (and to avoid bank charges). Any surplus funds should be placed on a deposit account so as to earn interest, although the banks are now moving to the situation where interest will be paid on current account too.

Monthly totalling of the cash analysis book is essential. The monthly totals should be made when the bank statements are received, and the totals will be adjusted to allow for any uncleared cheques. Thus, the owner is enabled to keep an eye on the financial health of the business. Most equine businesses will be registered for value added tax and this involves the regular submission of VAT returns to the Commissioners of Customs and Excise, usually accompanied by a payment of the difference between the VAT input tax (which has been charged to the business by suppliers) and the output tax (which has been charged by the business to its clients).

When ordering goods, after receiving and considering any quotations, an order is written and then the delivery note and invoice can be reconciled with the order. Payment is made by cheque and the amount is shown as an expense in the appropriate column of the cash analysis book. If goods are sold – a horse, for example – an invoice should be raised showing the amount of VAT. This is then entered as a receipt in the book. Any cash transactions, e.g. riding lessons, must also be recorded. A riding school dealing largely with cash clients should keep a till and check the takings at the end of each day. These are then paid into the bank on a regular basis, and the paying-in slip provides the record for the entry made in the cash analysis book. Payments should never be made from the till, but always from petty cash.

Two other areas are slightly more complex – veterinary expenses and farrier's charges. The best plan is to have a duplicate book for each of these kept in the yard, listing the horses and any treatment or shoeing. Each book is completed at the time of the visit, and the duplicate sheet is taken to the office to be reconciled with the account. The stable manager of a livery yard should keep similar books for recording things such as clipping and worming which are chargeable to the client. This procedure sounds complicated but is simple to operate in practice.

The end of the financial year

At the end of each financial year there are other accounting procedures to be carried out, usually by the accountant from the books and records kept by the business throughout the year: valuation, the profit and loss account, and the balance sheet.

Valuation

The whole business should be valued at the close of the year, usually on the last financial day of the year. Valuation means a formal assessment of the worth of the assets of the business, and starts off with an inventory. Valuation is a profession and so only general guidance can be given; the small business owner will rely on the accountant for advice because the tax implications of the net worth of the business must be borne in mind. The valuation should be realistic. Stock can be valued at the cost of production or at its estimated market value – the price it would fetch if sold in the open market under normal conditions. For tax purposes, if the actual costs of production cannot be accurately shown, the Inland Revenue authorities will usually allow stock which is to be sold on (trading livestock) to be valued at current market value, less an agreed percentage. If the value of stock is over-estimated (i.e. valued above what it cost to produce), the business will appear to be making a profit on paper, although the 'profit' will not in fact exist. It is foolish to value on the basis of anticipated profits. To avoid a 'paper profit' it is best to be conservative in valuing both young stock and competition animals. In valuing machines and implements, one starts with the previous year's total value, adds in the value of items purchased and deducts any items sold. An allowance is made for depreciation at the rate agreed with the accountant – and this is usually 25 per cent. Stores in stock are shown at cost price, regardless of current market value, e.g. hay in the barn is shown in the accounts at the price it was bought in at, regardless of any increase in value. Small items – such as bits – are usually 'written off' in the year of purchase.

Profit and loss account

The profit and loss (or trading) account is an important tool for financial management, and is based on the information provided by the cash analysis account. The opening valuation (the net worth of the business based on the previous year's valuation) is added to the sales and receipts, which are then balanced. If the purchases and expenses plus the opening valuation is the lower figure of the two, the difference is the net profit. If the sales and receipts plus the closing valuation is the lowest figure, the difference is the net loss.

The Balance Sheet

A complete financial picture at the end of each year is provided by the Balance Sheet:

Liabilities		Assets	
		Valuation of business	
Debts payable – goods and services received but not yet paid for, i.e. money owed to creditors	£	Debts due – goods and services sold but not yet paid for, i.e. money owed by debtors	£
Bank overdraft	£	Money in the bank	£
Borrowed money, e.g. mortgage debts	£	Cash in hand	£
Total Liabilities:	£____	Total Assets:	£____
	Net Capital Worth: £		

Assets and liabilities must balance. The point of the exercise is to establish the value of the business on the day, i.e. its net capital worth. If this comes to a negative figure, the business is insolvent.

5 The law

Introduction

A basic knowledge of business law is an essential part of management. 'Ignorance of the law is no excuse' and every aspect of business is affected by legal considerations. This chapter outlines some essential law.

English law consists of statute law – Acts of Parliament and regulations made under them such as the Importation of Equine Animals Order 1970 – and common law or case law. Common law is the rules and principles expressed in decisions of the courts over the centuries. Under the English system of case law, a judge is bound to decide a question in the way in which it has been decided previously by judges in one of the superior courts (the House of Lords, Court of Appeal or the High Court) in earlier cases. This is called the system of judicial precedent. Case law is a most important part of English law and grows on a daily basis.

For our purposes, there are two broad categories of law: civil (or private) law and criminal law. Civil law deals with the relationships between citizens; civil law duties can be enforced by litigation in a private action in the High Court or the County Court and are remedied by an order for the the payment of money compensation (damages) or some other remedy such as an injunction. In contrast, criminal law deals with offences against the public good and is enforced by prosecution by the State or its agents. If crime is established it can be punished by fine or imprisonment.

Civil law includes the law of contract and the law of tort, both of which are of great importance to owners of horse establishments. Contract deals with legally binding agreements between people, for example a contract of employment, a contract to buy a horse or a contract for the sale of land. The law of tort deals with civil wrongs where there is a breach of some duty imposed generally by the law. There are many types of torts such as negligence, trespass and private nuisance.

This chapter deals only in wide-ranging outline with some of the law affecting horse businesses. A useful book for reference is *Essential Law for Landowners and Farmers* by Michael Gregory and Margaret Parrish (2nd edition, Collins), but wherever there is a legal problem the advice of a competent solicitor should be obtained.

The law of contract

All businesses involve buying and selling and contracts for the sale of goods are the most frequent business transaction. Contrary to popular opinion, a contract does not normally need to be in writing or be supported by written evidence except in special cases. These cases apart, a verbal contract is valid and enforceable, and any dispute is decided on the basis of the evidence before the court. Documentary evidence is often desirable, but the majority of day-to-day contracts is made by word of mouth, e.g. having a riding lesson in return for a fee or buying a beer in a public house. Generally, then, a contract does not need to be in any particular form, but there are important exceptions such as contracts of hire-purchase. These must be made in writing in a prescribed form under the Consumer Credit Act 1974.

Detailed consideration of the general law of contract is outside the scope of this book, but since buying and selling is such an important part of any business activity, something must be said about the rules governing sales of goods. Contracts for the sale of goods do not need to be in writing. 'Goods' include horses and other livestock as well as inanimate objects such as hay, machinery, vehicles, etc. They are governed by the Sale of Goods Act 1979. Section 2(1) of the Act defines a contract for the sale of goods as one 'by which the seller transfers or agrees to transfer the property in goods to the buyer for a money consideration, called the price'. A sale of goods therefore involves three essential elements: (a) a contract (b) a transfer of goods and (c) the price.

A contract

A contract is a legally binding agreement made between two or more parties. It involves an offer made by one party, unconditionally accepted by the other party, and supported by consideration, i.e. the price. The agreement must not be uncertain in any way and the application of this rule gives rise to many difficulties in practice. In one case, for example, a theatre manager agreed to engage an actress 'at a West End salary to be agreed between us'. It was ruled that there was no binding contract unless and until the parties agreed the salary.

A transfer of goods

Section 61(1) of the Sale of Goods Act 1979 contains a very complex definition of the simple word 'goods'. It includes not only animals but also growing crops or anything else which is attached to land, but which it is agreed will be detached. A typical equestrian example is the purchase of hay from the field.

The price

This is the payment in exchange for the goods. Transfer of ownership in the goods does not depend on the actual payment of the price. Ownership passes from the seller to the buyer when the parties intend it to be transferred and they are free to make appropriate provision in the contract. If, as is usually the case in the horse world, the parties make no express provision, s. 18 of the 1979 Act lays down specific rules. Two of them are of particular importance. The basic rule is that where there is a contract for the sale of specific goods in a deliverable state, such as a horse, 'the property in the goods passes to the buyer when the contract is made, and it is immaterial whether the time of payment or the time of delivery, or both, is postponed'. In the normal case, therefore, the ownership is transferred when the bargain is struck.

A different rule applies where goods are delivered to the buyer on approval or on sale or return or other similar terms. In that case, ownership is transferred when the buyer signifies his approval or acceptance to the seller or does something else which makes it clear that he is adopting the transaction. The buyer cannot hold out indefinitely. If no time limit has been specified, then he must act within what lawyers call 'a reasonable time'.

The law *implies* certain terms to be performed by the seller into contracts for the sale of goods. A most important term, which cannot be excluded, is that the seller has the right to sell and that in the case of an agreement to sell, he has the right to do so at the time ownership passes to the buyer: 1979 Act, s. 12(1)(a). For example, if a client agrees to buy a horse from a dealer and nothing is said about ownership, the buyer can assume that the dealer owns the horse or has the right to sell as agent or will have that right when ownership is transferred.

This is a condition of the contract – a term of vital importance – and if the dealer did not have the right to sell, the buyer could repudiate the contract and recover the purchase price. In some cases he might also recover damages. In one case, a horse was sold by mistake at an auction.

The mistake was discovered and delivery of the horse was refused to the buyer. The auctioneer who had mistakenly sold the horse was held liable to pay damages to the buyer.

Another implied condition applies where there is a sale by description, e.g. a saddle described as 'a jumping saddle'. The goods must then comply with the description, i.e. the saddle must be cut for jumping. If the goods do not do so, the buyer can sue for damages: s. 13, 1979. The same rule applies where a horse is sold by description.

The common law rule of *caveat emptor* ('let the buyer beware') is restated by s. 14(1) of the 1979 Act. What it means is that the purchaser must be careful when buying goods and examine them for obvious defects. This basic rule applies to private sales but is modified for sales made *in the course of a business* when other terms are imposed. These cannot be excluded by the seller in 'consumer sales', i.e. sales made by a seller who is selling goods as a business to someone for his private use and who is not buying in the course of a business. The classic example is a sale of a horse by a dealer or a riding stables to a private client.

The conditions implied are: (a) merchantable quality (b) fitness for purpose and (c) sale by sample.

Merchantable quality

Goods sold must be of 'merchantable quality'. This is defined as being as 'fit for the purpose(s) for which goods of that kind are commonly bought as it is reasonable to expect having regard to any description applied to them, the price (if relevant) and all the other relevant circumstances': 1979 Act, s. 14(2). The requirement applies to both new and second-hand goods, although if goods are sold as second-hand, the buyer must expect goods of a lower standard.

The application of this rule to a sale of new goods is shown by a case in 1987 where a new Range Rover had a defective engine, gearbox, bodywork and oil seals. Each of these defects required repairs, but none of them made the vehicle unroadworthy or undrivable. It was nonetheless held that the vehicle was not of merchantable quality. The court rejected the argument that one should expect some defects in a new vehicle and that the Range Rover was not unmerchantable because there was a manufacturer's warranty. This was irrelevant to the contractual position between the buyer and the seller.

In another case, the contract was for the sale of a second-hand car. The engine failed after 2,300 miles of use by the buyer. The car was held not to have been of merchantable quality.

There are two exceptions to the rule about merchantable quality:

- It does not apply if the defects are drawn specifically to the buyer's attention before the contract is made.
- It does not apply where the buyer actually examines the goods before the contract is made as regards defects which his examination ought to reveal.

Fitness for purpose

If the buyer makes known to the seller the purpose for which the goods are required, either by telling him expressly or by implication, there is an implied condition that the goods will be fit for that purpose, unless the circumstances show that the buyer is not relying on the seller's skill or judgement or that it would be unreasonable for him to do so: 1979 Act, s. 14(3).

In the horse world, buyers often rely on the seller's skill and judgement when purchasing a horse. The purpose does not have to be explained to the buyer if it is obvious what the horse is going to be used for. Two examples illustrate the situation. A rider approaches a dealer and says that he requires a horse for jumping and is sold a horse that does not jump. There is a breach of the condition. A novice rider approaches the riding school where he is receiving lessons and says that he wants to buy a horse. He is sold a very fiery mount which is hard to control. There would again be a breach of the condition.

Sale by sample

Under s. 15 of the 1979 Act, where goods are ordered by reference to a sample, there is an implied condition that the bulk will correspond with the sample. The buyer must be given a reasonable opportunity to check this.

This rule is important when buying hay, straw and so on where there is often a sale by sample. If the bulk supplied is not of the right quality then the buyer can reject the goods and recover the purchase price.

The condition about title (s. 12) can never be excluded from a contract of sale. The last three conditions mentioned cannot be excluded by the seller in 'consumer sales' which is of importance to equestrian businesses who sell horses, etc. to clients as part of the business. It applies even if the business has only just started.

Express warranties and conditions

Apart from the terms implied by the Sale of Goods Act 1979, many sales of horses are subject to express warranties and undertakings given by the seller to the buyer. Statements that a horse is 'warranted sound', 'warranted sound in wind and limb', 'warranted as a good hunter', 'warranted free from vice' or 'warranted quiet in every way' are all express warranties. They are conditions of the contract. If the statements prove untrue, the condition is broken. The purchaser is then entitled to repudiate the contract within a reasonable time and get his money back on returning the horse and to claim damages. Express warranties only cover the position at the time of sale, but as will be seen there is a broad legal definition of 'unsoundness'. Case law establishes that the seller is liable if he warrants a horse as 'sound' and it later proves to be unsound because of some latent defect.

A warranty may be limited in time as is usually the case at auction sales of horses where there are special conditions covering warranties given in the catalogue descriptions or by the auctioneer. The usual condition is that notice of the alleged breach must be given within a short time period and that any dispute is to be decided by an independent veterinary surgeon. Once the period specified has elapsed, the right to complain of the breach of condition is lost. It is best to follow a similar practice if selling a horse in the course of one's own business.

There is a distinction between unsoundness and vice. Unsoundness is a question of usefulness and not of disease. In the words of a nineteenth century judge:

'The rule as to unsoundness is that if at the time of sale, the horse has any disease which either actually does diminish the natural usefulness of the animal, so as to make him less capable of work of any description or which in its ordinary progress will diminish the natural usefulness of the animal, or if the horse has, either from disease or accident undergone any alterations of structure that either actually does at the time, or in its ordinary effects will, diminish the natural usefulness of the horse, such a horse is unsound': Baron Parke in *Coates* v. *Stephens* (1838).

This old definition is important. In practice, it may be apparent that at the time of sale a horse has a disease or defect which diminishes its natural usefulness, but it is very difficult to establish whether a horse has some minor defect which may diminish its natural usefulness in the future which again makes the animal unsound. This is one of the reasons why veterinary surgeons do not like to certify a horse as 'sound'.

Broken wind, coughing, navicular disease, spavin and wind galls producing lameness have all been held to be instances of unsoundness, and there are many other instances.

A vice – contrasted with unsoundness – is a particular habit or temperament in the animal which is not ordinarily found in a horse, and which has the effect of rendering it dangerous or less useful or liable to suffer in health. Kicking and crib-biting are typical instances of vice.

Misrepresentation

In negotiations leading up to a sale, the seller often makes statements about his wares which do not become terms of the contract. Sometimes the statements are mere 'puffs' not intended to be taken seriously; in other cases there are statements of fact which are one of the significant inducing causes of the contract but which fall short of becoming terms of the contract. Untrue statements of this sort are called misrepresentations, and the party who has been misled may be able to claim damages and/or treat the contract as at an end if he can establish that he was induced to enter into the contract because of the misrepresentation. The misstatement must be one of fact, not of pure opinion or of law. But a seller cannot escape liability merely by prefacing his statement with 'I believe that', or 'In my opinion', especially where he is in the trade.

Misrepresentations are either fraudulent, innocent or negligent. A fraudulent misrepresentation is a false statement of fact made 'knowingly, or without belief in its truth, or recklessly, careless whether it to be true or false', i.e. dishonestly: *Derry* v. *Peek* (1889). Proving that a statement is fraudulent is difficult. A negligent misrepresentation is easier to establish. It is a careless statement of fact made in circumstances which make it likely that the other person will reasonably rely on it. This will invariably be the case where the seller of goods is a trader. An innocent misrepresentation is an untrue statement made without fault on the part of the maker.

A fraudulent misrepresentation entitles the innocent party to claim damages and to have the contract set aside. Alternatively, he may claim damages for deceit and affirm the contract. Someone who has been induced to enter into a contract by a negligent misrepresentation can set the contract aside on discovering the truth and/or claim damages. The maker of a negligent misrepresentation must pay damages unless he proves that he has reasonable grounds to believe and did believe up to the time the contract was made that the facts represented were true. If the contract is induced by an innocent misrepresentation, the person misled may also rescind the contract or obtain damages in lieu at the discretion of the court. There are some limits to the right to set the contract aside, but this is a broad summary of the position.

Contracts of employment

Contracts of employment can be entered into formally or informally. (An example of a formal contract is that for a working pupil, as discussed below.) They usually come about as a result of interviews as discussed in Chapter 3 when the parties should expressly agree the terms which form the basis of the contract: nature of the duties, hours of work, holidays, overtime, time off, sick pay and so on. If the employer provides facilities for an employee's property, e.g. car parking or a cloakroom, he cannot restrict his liability for death or injury resulting from negligence, and as a result of s. 2 of the Unfair Contract Terms Act 1977 he can only exclude or restrict his liability for damage to the employee's property by a term of the contract which is reasonable in all the circumstances.

Unless the employee works less than 16 hours a week or is the husband or wife of the employer, not later than the end of the thirteenth week from the commencement of employment, section 1 of the Employment Protection (Consolidation) Act 1978 requires the employer to give the employer a written statement containing the following information:

- The names of the parties.
- The date when the employment began and the date on which the employee's period of continuity of employment began (taking into account any previous employment with a previous employer).
- The rate or scale of remuneration or method of calculating it.
- The intervals at which it is to be paid, e.g. weekly or monthly.
- The terms and conditions relating to hours of work.
- Terms and conditions of holiday entitlement (including public holidays), holiday pay and accrued holiday pay.
- Details of any sick pay or pension rights.
- The length of notice which the employee must give and is entitled to receive.
- The title of the job the employee is employed to do.
- Whether the employment is contracted-out of the State Pensions Scheme.

This written statement is not the contract between the parties but is strong evidence of what the contract terms are. This statement should be prepared in duplicate and the employee should be asked to sign one copy which should be kept in his employment file. The statement must also include a note:

(a) specifying any disciplinary rules applicable to the employee or referring to a document such as a Staff Handbook which specifies those rules and which is reasonably accessible to him;
(b) specifying by name or description the person to whom he can apply if he feels dissatisfied with any disciplinary decision;
(c) specifying the person to whom he can apply if he has a grievance about his employment.

This is not as formidable as it sounds and printed pro-forma written particulars can be obtained from most stationers. What is more problematical is the fact that, whatever has been agreed about notice from the employer bringing the contract of employment to an end, all employees who have been continuously employed for more than one year are protected from *unfair dismissal*, which can occur even if the employer terminates the contract with notice or pay in lieu of notice. Every employee covered by the legislation has the right not to be unfairly dismissed, and the remedy is for him to complain to an industrial tribunal, which has power to award compensation. Although there is no dismissal if the employee agrees to resign, there will be a dismissal if an employee is threatened with dismissal unless he does resign.

There are five grounds on which a dismissal is capable of being fair:

- The reason relates to the capability or qualifications of the employee for performing the work of the kind which he was employed to do.
- It relates to the conduct of the employee.
- Redundancy. In this case the employee may be entitled to redundancy pay, the amount of which is dependent on age, length of service, and the amount of the weekly pay.
- Because the employee cannot continue to work in the position he held without contravening some statutory obligation, e.g. where an employee who is required to drive motor vehicles loses his driving licence.
- There is some other substantial reason justifying the dismissal.

Provided the dismissal is on one of these grounds and that the proper procedures have been observed so that there is a full investigation, a proper hearing, a right to appeal and so on (as set out in the ACAS Code of Practice, which is obtainable from Her Majesty's Stationery Office) the dismissal will be held to be fair. In reaching a decision to dismiss, the employer must consider all the circumstances. The dismissal will be fair if the employer has acted reasonably. *The Right to Dismiss*, Second Edition, by Michael Whincup (BSP) is a useful handbook for employers.

Working pupil contracts

The position of working pupils requires brief consideration as, despite trade union opposition to the working pupil arrangement, many riding schools and stables operate a working pupil scheme under which the establishment offers practical and theoretical tuition for examinations in return for fees and the working pupil carrying out specific duties. The unions' opposition to the system has some justification in practice because, in the past, the system has been abused and working pupils have been used as a form of cheap labour.

The British Horse Society has made various recommendations about the points which should be covered in a working pupil contract and agreed by the establishment and the pupil before the course commences. These recommendations are not mandatory and are merely a guide. The BHS suggest that the contract should include:

- a broad description of the duties which the working pupil is expected to perform;
- financial arrangements;
- details of any probationary period;
- hours of work;
- public and other holidays and time of, which should include weekends;
- the mounted and dismounted training which the working pupil will receive, including practical teaching experience;
- the examination for which the training will be given, its approximate date, and responsibility for making the entry;
- food and accommodation, including bedding, linen, etc.;
- keep of working pupil's horse (if any);
- competitions, hunting, etc;
- disciplinary rules, e.g. time-keeping, dress, etc. A working pupil contract should be entered into formally between the establishment and the student and his parents. A specimen contract is available from the British Horse Society.

The law of tort

A tort is a civil wrong other than a breach of contract or a breach of trust which gives rise to an action for damages or some other civil remedy. It is not a criminal wrong and is not punishable by the State. Each tort has developed separately and has its own characteristics and remedies. Important torts include negligence, trespass and private nuisance all of which are of importance to the occupier of land.

Negligence

Negligence in law is not the same as carelessness or mistake: it is conduct and not a state of mind. Negligence is the breach of a duty of care owed by one person to another which results in damage. It is the omission to do something that a reasonable man would do, or the doing of something that a prudent and reasonable man would not do. To succeed in an action for negligence, the plaintiff (claimant) must establish:

(a) that the defendant was under a duty of care owed to him. Everyone has a duty to take reasonable care not to harm others.
(b) that the defendant was in breach of that duty.
(c) that the plaintiff suffered foreseeable damage as a result. 'Damage' usually means physical harm to persons or property but in rare cases it can include purely financial loss.

There is a large and, unfortunately, fast growing body of case law dealing with negligence and there is no way in which an equestrian establishment can exclude or limit liability for *death or personal injury resulting from negligence* because of the provisions of the Unfair Contract Terms Act 1977 which is as crucial to tort as it is to contract. The Act applies to 'business liability', i.e. liability arising from 'things done or to be done by a person in the course of a business' and the occupation of premises used for 'business purposes'. Any contract term or notice purporting to exclude liability will be invalid. In the case of other loss caused by negligence, or death or personal injury resulting from a tort other than negligence, an exclusion or limitation of liability is a nullity unless it satisfies a vague test of 'reasonableness'. Clearly, then, the display by a Riding Establishment of a notice saying 'Clients ride entirely at their own risk' is ineffective to protect the proprietor. Warning notices are still desirable, however, as indicating that the owner of the business has acted prudently.

It is important to realise that an employer is vicariously liable for the actions of his employees acting in the course of employment even if the employee is acting in defiance of an express prohibition. Adequate insurance cover against civil liability is therefore essential.

Voluntary assumption of risk

The Latin maxim *volenti non fit injuria* (where there is consent there is no injury) provides a very limited defence to an action in tort in very special circumstances. Those who take part in a sport or pastime are sometimes taken to have accepted the risk of dangers which are incidental to the ordinary conduct of the pastime. It must be established that the claimant freely and voluntarily assumed the risk, with the full knowledge of its nature and extent. The maxim has little or no application to actions by employees against employers because a person employed as a servant who accepts a risk incidental to his employment is not to be treated as accepting it voluntarily. The 1977 Act previously discussed further restricts its operation. In one case in 1962 it was applied where a non-paying spectator was injured by a horse competing at a jumping show. The rider was not liable even though he committed an error of judgement.

The Occupiers' Liability Acts 1957 and 1984

Negligence is generally applicable to activities being carried out on a property. These statutes set out the legal duty owed by the occupier of premises to 'visitors' (as defined) and to 'persons other than his visitors'. They are concerned with premises which are dangerous because they are in defective or dangerous state. In some cases an injured person can sue alternatively for negligence and breach of the Act. The word 'premises' is defined in very wide terms and means the property of the occupier, including fixed or movable structures.

The 1957 Act applies to lawful visitors 'using the premises' and covers people entering with permission or at the invitation of the occupier, as well as people entering as of right such as the host of officials empowered by statute to enter premises. Permission may be express or implied, and so the definition covers all people lawfully on the property. Other entrants *including trespassers* are covered by the 1984 Act.

The 1957 Act provides that the occupier owes a 'common duty of care' to all visitors except to the limited extent he can modify it by agreement. Section 2(2) defines the duty owed in these terms:

'The common duty of care as a duty to take such care as in all the circumstances of the case is reasonable to see that the visitor will be reasonably safe in using the premises for the purposes for which he is invited or permitted by the occupier to be there.'

Whether the standard required has been attained is a question of fact; the Act requires occupiers to act reasonably. The occupier must be prepared for children to be less careful than adults and what is not a danger to an adult may be a danger to a child. Adult visitors are expected to take reasonable care of themselves and where someone comes on to the property to exercise his calling, e.g. a window cleaner, may be expected to appreciate and guard against any special risks ordinarily incidental to his job. If there are dangers on the premises the occupier should guard them. Visitors' attention should be drawn to any special or hidden dangers by suitable notices or other means. A warning does not of itself absolve from liability but will be taken into account in deciding whether the occupier is liable for a mishap.

Liability to trespassers and other uninvited entrants is regulated by s. 1 of the 1984 Act. A duty is owed to uninvited entrants 'to take such care as is reasonable in all the circumstances of the case to see that he does not suffer injury (i.e. death or physical or mental injury, not property damage) on the premises by reason of the danger concerned' if three conditions are met:

(1) The occupier knows of the danger or has reasonable grounds to believe it exists.
(2) He knows, or has reasonable grounds to believe, that the entrant either is or might come into the vicinity of the danger.
(3) The risk of injury resulting from the danger is one against which in all the circumstances of the case the occupier can reasonably be expected to offer the uninvited entrant some protection.

A significant difference between the common duty of care owed under the 1957 Act to visitors and the duty under the 1984 Act is that the latter can 'in an appropriate case, be discharged by taking such steps as are reasonable in all the circumstances of the case to give warning of the danger concerned or to discourage a person from incurring risk'. All this is very vague and while a plain warning notice might well discharge liability to adult trespassers, it would probably be ineffective in the case of mischievous children.

The Animals Act 1971

People who own and control animals are under the same duty of care as those responsible for anything else. In one case, for example, the defendant was held liable when his unattended pony became restive and grabbed at a passing pedestrian and dragged her down. Most of the law about liability for animals is now found in the Animals Act 1971, which imposes strict liability (i.e. liability without fault) on the keeper of an animal of a 'dangerous species' for any damage done by it. A dangerous species is one which is not commonly domesticated in the British Isles, and whose fully grown animals have such characteristics that they are likely, unless restrained, to cause severe damage or that any damage they may cause is likely to be severe.

Of more interest to the horse business is the liability imposed in certain circumstances for an animal which does not belong to a dangerous species: s. 2(2), 1971 Act. Horses and ponies fall into this grouping. Liability is imposed regardless of fault provided three requirements are met:

- The damage must be of a kind which the animal was likely to cause if not restrained, or which if caused by the animal was likely to be severe.
- The likelihood of the damage or its being severe must be due to characteristics of the animal which are not normally found in animals of the same species except at particular times or in particular circumstances.
- Those characteristics must be known to the keeper of the animal or his employee or to a member of his household over 16.

The situation is illustrated by a case in 1962, where a groom recovered damages from the employer where a horse of unpredictable and unreliable behaviour crushed her against the bar of its trailer. The horse, a thoroughbred show jumper, had no previous tendency to injure people, but the judge found that its characteristics were of a kind not normally found in horses and that its keeper knew all about its characteristics.

Section 4 of the Animals Act 1971 also imposes strict liability for damage done by straying livestock which trespass on to someone else's land. Livestock means cattle, horses, asses, mules, hinnies, sheep, pigs, goats and poultry, as well as deer not in the wild state. The liability is for damage done by the livestock to the land or any property on it, but not personal injuries. Liability is strict; no fault has to be proved, but if the damage is the fault of the person suffering it there is no liability. However, it is the animals' owner's obligation to keep his livestock in and not the responsibility of other owners to keep them out. It is also a defence that the livestock strayed from the highway and its presence there was a lawful use of the highway.

The person trespassed against has the right to detain and eventually sell livestock which stray on his land, and its owner is liable to pay any expenses incurred in his doing so.

Section 8(1) of the 1971 Act imposes a duty of care to prevent animals straying on to the highway, but liability is not strict. The owner is not liable unless he has failed to exercise reasonable care to prevent his livestock straying, e.g. by fencing. But it is not a breach of the duty of care to place animals on unfenced common land where fencing is not customary, e.g. in the exercise of grazing rights on Dartmoor. If animals lawfully on the highway stray from it and cause damage, negligence must also be proved.

Trespass to land

Direct entry on to someone else's land without consent or lawful authority is trespass. Mistake, as such, is no defence to trespass. The occupier may sue even if no damage is done but this is seldom worthwhile. If a trespasser declines to leave the land when asked to do so, the law allows the occupier to eject the trespasser using no more force than is reasonably necessary, but it is very unwise to resort to self-help.

Private nuisance

A private nuisance is a state of affairs which has been defined by the courts as 'an unlawful interference with a person's use or enjoyment of land or some right over or in connection with it'. The interference must be substantial and in general actual damage must be proved. Excessive noise, fumes, smells and so on have all been held to amount to nuisances; a muck heap might be held to amount to a nuisance as might the noise and smell from horses or other animals. Much depends on the character of the locality: in country districts some noise and smell from animals must be tolerated. But it is a question of degree and in one case a pig farmer used a field near a housing estate for the deposit of pig excrement.

Much of the field was covered with slurry to a depth depth of 1 to 1.5 inches and the tipping had been carried out within close proximity of the windows of the houses causing personal discomfort to residents. This was held to amount to a nuisance. In essence whether or not something amounts to a nuisance is a matter of reasonableness and common sense. The characteristic remedy for private nuisance is an action for damages although the court may also grant an injunction which is an order to stop the nuisance.

Nuisance and trespass do not overlap, but there is an overlap between private nuisance and the rule in *Rylands* v. *Fletcher* (1886) which imposes strict liability on an occupier who brings something onto his land or accumulates it there and it escapes and causes damage. The bulk storage of water and the like has been held to be a 'non-natural use of land' for the purposes of the rule. There are very few defences to an action brought for damage caused by the escape.

(*Note*: Local authorities have powers to deal with 'statutory nuisances' by serving abatement notices enforced by orders made by the magistrates' court.)

The Riding Establishments Acts 1964 and 1970

Any equestrian establishment which hires out horses or gives riding lessons by way of business falls under this legislation, even if the activity is carried out only part-time. A licence must be obtained from the district council and the applicant must meet a number of conditions:

- The applicant must be a body corporate or at least 18 years of age.
- The applicant must not be disqualified from keeping a riding stable, a dog, pet shop, boarding kennels or from having custody of animals.
- The applicant must satisfy the local authority of his suitability and qualifications by examinations or experience to run a riding establishment. If he holds an 'approved certificate' (such as even an Assistant Instructor's Certificate of the BHS), the need to prove experience of horse management is dispensed with.

Licences are granted on a provisional (three months) and annual basis, and before issuing the licence there is an inspection of the premises. The district council must take various matters into account in deciding whether or not to grant the licence, all of which are for the welfare and benefit of the horses: see Table 5.1.

Table 5.1 Matters which must be considered in deciding whether to grant a licence for a riding establishment.

Regard must be had to the need for securing that:

- Paramount consideration will be given to the condition of the horses and that they will be maintained in good health and in all respects physically fit.
- In the case of a horse kept for letting on hire or being used to provide riding instruction it will be suitable for its purpose.
- The feet of all animals are properly trimmed and that, if shod, the shoes are properly fitted and in good condition.
- There will be available at all times accommodation for horses which is suitable as respects size, construction, number of occupants, lighting, ventilation, drainage in both new and converted buildings.
- Where horses are kept at grass there will be available to them at all times adequate pasture, shelter and water and required supplementary feed.
- Horses will be adequately supplied with suitable food, drink and bedding material (if stabled).
- Horses will be adequately exercised, groomed and rested and visited at suitable intervals.
- All reasonable precautions will be taken to prevent and control the spread of infectious or contagious diseases among horses.
- Veterinary first aid equipment and medicines will be provided and maintained at the premises.
- Appropriate steps will be taken for the protection and extrication of horses in case of fire and in particular the name, address and telephone number of the licence holder or some other responsible person will be prominently displayed outside the premises.
- Instructions as to action to be taken in the event of fire will similarly be kept displayed.
- Adequate accommodation will be provided for forage, bedding, stable equipment and saddlery.

The council may impose conditions to ensure that these requirements are met. Other basic conditions are:

- A horse found by an inspector to be in need of veterinary attention must not be returned to work until the licence owner has obtained and lodged with the council a veterinary certificate that the horse is fit for work.
- A horse must not be let out on hire for riding or used for providing riding instruction unless supervised by a responsible person aged over 15 unless the licence holder is satisfied that the hirer is competent to ride without supervision.

- There must always be a responsible person of at least 16 years of age in charge of the establishment during business hours.
- The licence holder must hold a current insurance policy covering him for personal injuries sustained by hirers or paying pupils and against injury to third parties arising from the hire or use of the horses.
- There must be a register of all horses in the licence holder's possession aged three years and under and usually kept on the premises. This register must be available for inspection by an authorised officer of the council at all times.

The annual inspections of most local authorities are very thorough, and the inspector (an authorised veterinary surgeon or veterinary practitioner) is empowered to inspect any premises in the district council's area where there is a licensed establishment or an establishment which has applied for a licence or where there is reason to believe that a person is keeping a riding establishment. This power is exercisable at all 'reasonable times'. Operating an unlicensed riding establishment is a criminal offence.

There are various other offences under the Acts. On conviction, the magistrates may fine or imprison the offender, and also disqualify the offender from holding a riding establishment licence.

The provisions of the Riding Establishments Acts are unremarkable. What is remarkable is the fact that the legislation does not extend to cover all equestrian businesses, but only that of keeping horses for either the purpose of letting them out for hire or for use in giving riding instruction for payment or both, e.g. it does not cover stables which provide only livery. The Acts also place no restrictions on the number of hours which horses may work, though some local authorities restrict the hours by means of a special condition in the licence. There is also pressure for the Act to be amended in respect of both the age of the person left in charge and the qualifications of the licence holder.

The Health and Safety at Work Act 1974

The need for compliance with health and safety legislation has already been discussed in Chapter 3. The 1974 Act (and the regulations made under it) are of great importance. It applies to people, not premises, and covers all employed persons (except domestic employees) wherever they work. Its provisions apply to trainees on government-sponsored training schemes (e.g. YTS) as if they were employees. The Act also applies to those who are not employees in so far as they may be affected by work activities.

The emphasis of the Act is on criminal sanctions and it is enforced on equestrian premises by the Agricultural Inspectorate, who have power to enter premises at any reasonable time or, if there is a dangerous situation, to enter at any time.

Two important weapons available to the inspectorate are improvement notices and prohibition notices.

- An *improvement notice* can be served where the inspector forms the opinion that someone is contravening a statutory provision and that the contravention is likely to be continued or repeated. It requires the named person to remedy the contravention within a specified period, which must not be less than 21 days.
- A *prohibition notice* can be issued if the inspector thinks that a work activity is being carried on in contravention of statute so as to involve a risk of serious personal injury. It stops the activity being carried on and can take immediate effect if the inspector forms the opinion that the risk of serious personal injury is imminent, otherwise its operation may be deferred until the end of a specified period. Prohibition orders can be issued on persons, e.g. for a failure to wear prescribed protective clothing.

Appeals against these notices can be made to an industrial tribunal on very limited grounds. Failure to comply with a valid notice is a serious criminal offence.

There is, of course, much other relevant law, but more detailed treatment is outside the scope of this book.

Further reading

Gregory, Michael and Parrish, Margaret (1987). *Essential Law for Landowners and Farmers*. Second Edition. London: Collins.

Powell-Smith, Vincent (to be published in 1990). *Essential Law for Horseowners*. Oxford: BSP Professional Books.

Shrubsall, Vivien (1989). *Contracts of Employment*. Oxford: BSP Professional Books.

Whincup, Michael (1987). *The Right to Dismiss*. Second Edition. Oxford: BSP Professional Books.

6 Finance and profit

Raising money

Every business needs capital, and in most cases this means borrowing money. There is no shortage of institutions prepared to lend money, and the method chosen will depend on a variety of factors. The most important of these are size of loan, length of repayment period and the cost.

Mortgages

You can take out a mortgage to buy a business or agricultural property. The mortgage – a charge on the property – is the security for the loan, the amount of which is limited not only by the value of the property but by what you can afford realistically to repay. Mortgage loans are available through the Agricultural Mortgage Corporation or through one of the several mortgage companies. The clearing banks are also willing to consider mortgages. An ordinary building society mortgage is not available for commercial enterprises. In any case, you will need some capital of your own to set up in business, whether this involves buying a property or not. No lender is going to advance 100 per cent of the total purchase price and costs involved.

A comparison should be made on terms – some lenders make a charge for arranging a mortgage and interest rates can vary. Some investors will offer to purchase a property and then lease it back to its former owner who gets the immediate capital injection needed for business purposes but forfeits the opportunity of increasing his capital worth if the property rises in value. Mortgages are for long-term finance; repayment terms of 10 and 20 years are common.

Those who are renting property will need to seek other sources of finance and will have to accept loans which are repayable over a shorter term – usually five years at the most. The most accessible source of finance is the clearing bank where you have your current account; even they will negotiate on terms if really pressed. There are several different types of bank credit, including overdrafts and loans of various sorts which can be used to finance a business. However, you will have to convince the bank manager not only of your creditworthiness but also that the venture is likely to succeed. This means that you must be able to present a good case to him, which in turn involves hard preparatory work.

The bank manager will need to know about you and your commitments and about your knowledge and business experience. Above all, he will need to be be satisfied that your plan is realistic and likely to succeed. You must convince him that there is a market and that you have the knowledge, enthusiasm and ability to succeed.

The bank's primary objective in lending money is to make a profit. The sensible bank manager will insist on seeing a realistic cash flow forecast and budget for at least the forthcoming year. This should show expected receipts and payments (including VAT), private drawings, bank charges and so on. This is certainly essential when embarking on a new venture, but in the case of an established business the audited accounts for the previous years can be used as the basis of your approach. Optimism and enthusiasm are insufficient; the project must be commercially viable.

Overdrafts

Overdrafts are one of the cheapest forms of borrowing and are intended for short-term loans. If the bank manager agrees to your request for an overdraft, you will be able to overdraw your current account up to an agreed limit. The amount and the length of the loan is a matter for his discretion – but an overdraft is not meant as a source of long-term finance. A bank manager will usually agree an overdraft facility against a realistic business plan showing clearly when the overdraft will be repaid, e.g. that a horse which is being brought on will be sold in the autumn. Interest is only payable for the period you are actually overdrawn and is between 2 and 5 per cent above the bank's base rate. Interest paid on an overdraft or loan for business purposes may be offset against the business's tax liability.

Ordinary loans

Unlike an overdraft, an ordinary loan must be repaid in regular amounts over an agreed period. The usual maximum is seven years. Typically, interest is only payable on the actual balance outstanding. Security such as an insurance policy may be required for substantial loans. The interest rate is similar to that charged on an overdraft.

Personal loans

The rate of interest on personal loans is fixed at the outset, and the term of the loan is usually two or three years. Personal loans are agreed for a specific purpose and in most cases security is not required although the bank may insist on your taking out life insurance in conjunction with the personal loan so as to ensure its repayment if you die.

Alternatives

Finance houses provide funds for hire purchase or credit sale to enable you to buy a specific piece of equipment or a vehicle. Some finance houses will also provide personal loans, but almost invariably they require security. With hire-purchase, in law you are hiring the goods. They do not become your property until the final instalment is paid. Repayments are normally spread over a maximum period of three years. Hire-purchase is a very expensive form of credit. Instalment repayments also apply where there is a credit sale, but in this case you become the owner of the goods immediately. There is also a form of credit known as 'conditional sale' which is similar to hire-purchase.

Grant aid

The most valuable source of extra capital is grant aid because this does not need to be given back.

Also, grant aid will in some circumstances supplement income for a person starting a new business. Some grants come from the European Economic Community (EEC) but most come from the Government.

Grants vary from area to area and in some grants are very specifically targeted at areas of need. To make the most of grant opportunities it is necessary to consult experts who are up to date with current provisions. The two organisations most likely to help a horse business with specialist knowledge of relevant grants are the Agricultural Development and Advisory Service (ADAS) and the Rural Development Commission (formerly CoSIRA); both have regional offices.

Budgeting

A budget is a *plan* of income and expenditure in contrast to accounts, which are a *record* of what has actually happened financially. A budget is a useful financial tool. For example, a buyer wishes to purchase a young horse and bring it on. He has a choice between buying an unbroken horse and having it broken professionally or of buying one that is already broken.

A simple budget of what it will cost to have the horse broken might look like this:

Transport to and from breaking yard	£ 20
6 weeks' livery at £70 per week	£420
Vet, farrier, clipping, etc.	£ 60
Total cost of breaking	£500

On this basis, the buyer can reach a sensible decision provided the estimated costs are accurate.

Similarly, a breeder will need to know when best to sell young stock and the price to ask. A budget can indicate the cost of producing each foal. This might work out as follows:

Depreciation of mare (purchased for £1250; final sale £250 divided by 5 foals)	£ 200
Mare's keep (say 5 foals over 7 years at £400/year)	£ 560
Getting mare in foal	
Stud fee £300	
Livery £150	£ 450
Veterinary expenses	£ 50
Weaning and sale preparation	£ 40
Cost of foal	£1300

If the breeder is an owner-occupier, the value of the property is probably an appreciating asset and so no charge need be made against the foal in the budget. In contrast, if the breeder is a tenant then the cost of (say) 2 acres would need to be added to the budget costs in order to achieve a realistic figure. This budget does not take account of any labour costs associated with the mare and foal. It also assumes that there is no bank overdraft or other finance charge. If labour costs and bank charges are involved, these will need to be allowed for in the budget. Thus, dependent on the breeder's circumstances, the foal must be sold for between £1700 and £2500 minimum in order to show a gross profit.

To keep the foal on instead of selling it immediately might result in the following pattern, assuming that the foal costs £400 a year for keep:

Foal	£1400
Yearling	£1800
2 year old	£2200
3 year old	£2600
4 year old	£3000

The breeder's dilemma is to decide the point at which the horse may be most profitably sold. In practice, the solution may be to produce the horse under saddle and then sell it; but this increases the risk element in the enterprise. The budget provides some information on which to make a decision.

Another situation arises where the owner of a new livery yard is considering what weekly livery fee to charge. One method of setting the rate would be to consider the charges made by other livery stables in the locality, compare standards and convenience, allow something for breaking into the market, and set the price accordingly. The second way is to prepare a budget and itemise the weekly costs associated with each horse. For example:

Cost of box (rent or maintenance and depreciation)	£ 7
Labour (self + 2 staff do 15 horses)	£25
Hay (bought from field)	£ 5
Concentrates (based on home-rolled barley)	£ 5
Bedding (shavings to save labour)	£ 5
Stable equipment, electricity and miscellaneous	£ 3
Total weekly cost	£50

To this basic figure, a profit margin must be added so as to produce the weekly charge to clients for each horse at livery.

Budgeting is thus a useful management tool for setting prices, comparing enterprises, making financial decisions and future projections; such budgets are called partial budgets. An overall budget for a project should be comprehensive and have a separate entry for as many items as possible. At the end of the budget period for the enterprise – usually a year – the budget should be compared with what actually happened.

Gross margins

An entrepreneur may be faced with a choice of two enterprises which are equally suited to his holding and must decide which enterprise is the more viable. One method of doing this is to look at the gross margins of each enterprise and compare them with a standard. The standard is usually taken to be the average of well-run similar enterprises. Because the basic costs (including labour) would remain the same whichever choice is made, they are excluded from gross margin calculations. The calculation is:

OUTPUT   minus   VARIABLE COSTS   = GROSS MARGIN

(Sales minus   (Feed, bedding, vet, etc.
depreciation of   plus extra casual labour)
livestock)

The concept of gross margin is a useful management tool well suited to agriculture and related businesses. Published statistical data on agriculture give average and above average performance figures for different enterprises ranging through the whole spectrum of farming activity. This information is set out in the *Farm Management Pocket Book* which is updated regularly and can be purchased from Wye College, Ashford, Kent TN25 5AH.

When using gross margin figures, it is important to remember that the published standards are only averages based on many holdings in different areas. Although the data is kept up to date, local conditions, seasons, market fluctuations and other factors will influence the actual performance of a holding. It must also be remembered that gross margins do not represent profit figures because the so-called 'fixed costs' such as rent, labour and general overheads must be deducted before arriving at a profit figure. This is done by constructing a partial budget as shown in the following example for putting a new enterprise in place of an old one:

Gross margin for new enterprise	£9,000	
Plus fixed costs saved	£1,500	
		£10,500
Less:		
Gross margin from old enterprise	£6,000	
Plus extra fixed costs	£2,000	
		−£8,000
Extra profit		£2,500

Gross margins are not only useful for planning; they can also be used to compare actual performance achieved with the performance of similar enterprises elsewhere.

In recent years, farm incomes have been falling steadily. The situation now in western Europe is that more food is produced than is required. It is too expensive to transport this food to underdeveloped countries and such an expedient might prove to be counter-productive in the long term. It is generally thought best to give underdeveloped countries assistance to make them self-sufficient. Because of the European food surplus, farmers are being encouraged to produce less food, and in order to increase income they are now being forced to look at new enterprises. Forestry is very slow and speciality enterprises such as herbs and venison offer only limited opportunities for a few. Farm gate sales and 'pick-your-own' ventures will continue to be useful, but the likelihood is that a great many farms will turn to the leisure industry. Probably the best hope for farmers lies in a national campaign of 'Riding for All'. The Government is already offering grants to help farmers establish livery businesses and the restriction on cereals policy will provide more land to ride. Farmers are making efforts to diversify so as to make up the shortfall.

Fortunately, there is now a reference handbook for farmers, advisers and all seeking to go into the horse business or improve the efficiency of existing businesses. The *Horse Business Management Reference Handbook* is published by Warwickshire College, Moreton Morrell, Warwick CV35 9BL. It gives figures based on a major national survey updated to reflect current costs and prices. Using the handbook as a reference, a horse business can review its own performance and compare it with other similar enterprises. The comparison will suggest areas for economy and increased output and perhaps enterprises which need discontinuing or radical alteration. It can also be of help in indicating suitable enterprises for exploration.

Facility uptake

Any business must be so managed that it earns its maximum potential, whether it be in terms of staff, stables, horses or any other asset. This is what 'facility uptake' is about. A horse business may have various facilities available, but not all of them may be used to full capacity. The facilities are there, but are not taken up by clients. For example, if a livery yard has twenty boxes, and there is an average of 10 horses in the yard at any one time, there is only a facility uptake of 50 per cent. The answer to this problem may lie in cutting the price or, more probably, in better marketing. Again, the working capacity of an instructor teaching five hours daily for five days a week would be 25 hours. However, if the instructor is fully worked for only two days and instructs for only 5 hours in total over the remaining working days, he is working at only 40 per cent of capacity. The teaching facility and the instructor's capacity is underused. The promotion of mid-week riding could alter the situation. Campaigns can be targeted at housewives and evening rides could be advertised so as to promote a better facility uptake. If evening rides provided the solution, then staff involved would need to be given adequate time off to compensate them for the evening work.

The use of an indoor school provides another example. An indoor school is an expensive capital item and therefore must be used for the maximum number of hours. A local competition horse trainer might be glad to use the school for an hour a day while the resident staff are at lunch. Livery owners might like to have an arrangement to use the school regularly while the staff are having a rest period. A local dog training group might be glad to use the school for one evening, and a local archery group on another. Such users not only provide income by paying for the use of the school, but if vending machines are installed, they will also use them and provide extra income. Moreover, by visiting the establishment regularly for their own purposes, they may well be tempted to ride.

Profitability

Not all equine businesses are profitable. Agriculture again provides some useful lessons because it is also concerned with livestock. An analysis of a group of farms has established that a very small change in either output (productivity) or a reduction in costs will have a large effect on profitability. These minor changes can pass unnoticed until they are forced into focus by a reduction in profit.

For example, for every £100 of costs in the sample group, if average output was £120, but some members received £130 and others only £110, the difference in profitability between these is a variation of the lower group earning only half the average income and the upper group earning 50 per cent more than average. Therefore, for the lower group, an 8 per cent improvement in performance could double the profitability of the business. A small reduction in costs would produce equally dramatic results.

The performance of every aspect of an equestrian business must therefore be scrutinised carefully so as to see if the output and cost ratios can be increased and decreased. Poor performance – for example, too many mares not in foal on a stud farm or too many ponies at a trekking centre for the number of clients – are easy to spot as indicators of poor management, as are extravagance and wastefulness. An apparently well-managed establishment with excellent performance which is not making an adequate profit may be buying the results at too high a cost. Comparison against standard data and a careful analysis of each enterprise should help to identify this type of problem. The cause may of course be that the total output of the holding is insufficient to meet the owner's needs. If this is the case, the owner must set about increasing output, e.g. by creating new enterprises.

Business management advisors in agriculture – such as those from the Agricultural Development and Advisory Service (ADAS) – are able to use established efficiency measures and have a host of comparative data on which to base comparisons. The horse industry is less fortunate since it has always been secretive about its figures. Modern equine businesses must therefore rely on maintaining good records and making comparisons of performance from year to year against such published data as there is.

A riding school can measure earnings per horse. A stud farm can measure foals weaned against the number of mares owned. As horse people become more conscious of performance details and make comparisons with published data, so management in the industry will become more sophisticated in spotting the strengths and weaknesses of the system.

Economies of scale

Economies of scale can contribute substantially to profitability, and this includes buying in bulk. Bulk buying may involve tying up capital or even obtaining a loan, but nonetheless the saving will justify the costs.

The feed bill is the first area for economy. Barley bought directly from a farmer can be stored in bulk provided it is sufficiently dry. The store must be either a hopper on legs which is filled by a bulk tanker lorry or the store will require a grain auger to carry the feed upwards. In smaller establishments, the alternative is for the grain to be put up in a bucket. The grain from the bulk store can then be rolled each week to meet the yard's needs.

Feed mills sell mixer rations of high protein food designed to be mixed with barley. Horse feed nuts tend to be very expensive and horses do well on low protein dairy nuts, which are cheaper. Some cattle (beef) nuts contain substances which are poisonous to horses and so care must be taken when choosing nuts.

When purchasing feed direct from merchants, the total quantity of feed can be estimated by type and quotations for the year's supply can be obtained from competing merchants. Considerable variation will be found in the quotations.

Hay can be purchased direct from the field and is thus handled less often. (The more often fodder is handled, the more it will cost!) Moreover, as winter progresses the price of hay increases. The best possible price is obtained by buying all the hay needed for the season at one time. The safe maxim is 'the larger the quantity, the keener the price'.

Agricultural merchants do not necessarily expect to get the marked price for each item they display when purchases are made in reasonable quantity. Items such as wheelbarrows, buckets, brooms, fencing materials and so on can often be purchased at a discounted price.

Tack shops operate on a mark-up of 100 per cent. There is thus some room for negotiation when a tack shop wishes to secure the business of a horse establishment. Even the farrier and the vet are in business and so it is wise to discuss with them what economies can be made so as to keep their accounts at a tolerable level.

The cost of bedding is also worth considering. If straw is used, it costs less from the field. However, wood shavings offer economies in labour and a simple budget will readily show the labour saved against the extra cost of the shavings. If the number of horses and the number of staff remain unchanged, no real saving will be made by changing from straw to shavings, but if an extra horse can be kept with the same staff then a saving is achieved.

Taxation

The first essential for any business is a competent bank manager who can advise on the best sources of finance and help with the financial planning. The second essential is a competent business advisor. The bank manager may double in this role or the advisor may be an independent professional consultant or someone from ADAS or the Rural Development Commission. The third essential is a good accountant. He is not only concerned with auditing but will also ensure that money is not going unnecessarily from the business into the government coffers through the overpayment of tax. The cost of any professional advice is small when compared with the actual and potential savings.

All the advisors should be interested in the business and visit the premises. They should be regarded as friends who are concerned to see the business go from strength to strength. Because grants and taxation change each year, these professionals will keep the business in line with any fiscal opportunities. The owner of the business will certainly need his accountant to advise on and monitor those expenses which can legitimately be offset as business expenses and also to suggest the optimum times for major capital expenditure.

The accountant should advise on and agree to the book-keeping system, since he will have to audit the accounts. The simpler and better kept the system is, the quicker (and cheaper) it will be to carry out the annual audit.

The accountant will also be able to give advice about the legal form the business should take – sole trader, partnership or private limited liability company. The principal advantage of a limited liability company is that the liability of the shareholders is limited to the nominal value of the shareholding. If things go wrong the shareholders are not liable to the full extent of their assets if the venture fails because the limited company is a separate legal entity with assets of its own. Another advantage of trading as a limited company is that the owner(s) of the business can become salaried employees of the company as directors. As employees they may be eligible for Social Security benefits (including unemployment pay) if things go wrong. In the case of a sole trader or a partnership, if the business fails and has substantial liabilities, the individual sole trader or partners carry unlimited liability which extends to all personal assets. In the worst case, a sole trader or member of a partnership can be made bankrupt and lose everything, including their home. Insolvency law treats debtors harshly, even if there is no personal fault. However, there may be tax advantages in being self-employed and operating as a sole trader or as a member of a partnership. In every case an accountant's advice should be obtained before deciding on the best sort of business arrangement.

Table 6.1 shows the taxes to be dealt with.

The Inland Revenue compels employers to deduct Schedule E income tax from staff wages each week on the pay as you earn (PAYE) system, together with National Insurance contributions at the appropriate rate. These sums are then sent by the employer to the local income tax office. The Inland Revenue provide employers with the necessary documentation but the system is very complicated and time-consuming. Some people leave the mechanics of PAYE to their accountant; others buy

Table 6.1 Taxation.

---

(1) Income tax
- (a) Personal
  - (i) PAYE – for regular employees.
  - (ii) Schedule D – for self-employed.
- (b) Business (company) – 'corporation tax'.

(2) Capital tax
- (a) Capital gains tax.
- (b) Inheritance tax (has replaced capital transfer tax).

(3) Value added tax

(4) Special taxes
- (a) Stamp duty.
- (b) Car tax.
- (c) Petrol tax.
- (d) Excise duty on alcohol.

(5) Poll tax (to replace domestic rates)

---

computer payroll packages which are annually up-dated.

Taxable income is not the same as gross income, and there are various allowances which are set against the gross income so as to arrive at the taxable income. The Inland Revenue will advise the employer of the employee's individual coding which will take the allowances into account (e.g. a single person has a personal allowance) so that income tax is only deductible on earnings above this amount.

Value added tax (VAT) may also have to be contended with. All businesses with a turnover above the prescribed limit must be registered for VAT with the Commissioners of Customs and Excise. As its name suggests, value added tax is charged to the customers by the business on its sales and services ('output tax'), and then remitted to the Customs and Excise, usually on a quarterly basis. However, the business is entitled to offset against the output tax the VAT which it has paid on purchases and services ('input tax'). Smaller businesses which operate below the VAT registration limit have an advantage over their VAT-registered competitors when offering livery or other services or selling horses.

One of the advantages of a do-it-yourself (DIY) livery yard is that the clients buy all the necessary feed themselves – usually from the owner of the livery stable – and since animal food is zero rated (i.e. not subject to VAT) the customer saves. Customers may achieve a further saving if, for example, a husband runs a livery business as one entity and his wife runs a feed sale business as another, and the turnover of the livery business is below the VAT level.

Under certain conditions of sale, VAT-registered horse dealers need charge VAT only on their profit and not on the full selling price. This is as a result of the so-called 'second-hand scheme'. The scheme applies to sales from private individuals or from those in business who have sold under the 'margin' scheme. Animals are not eligible if they are being sold for the first time, have been imported by the dealer himself or have been purchased from someone who charged VAT on the full selling price or showed VAT separately on his invoice. Sales must be documented on a special form obtainable at small charge from the British Equestrian Trade Federation, Wothersome Grange, Bramham, near Wetherby, Yorkshire LS23 6LY which administers the scheme and from which detailed information can be obtained.

Another tax to be considered is the poll tax which is replacing domestic rates. Industrial rates will not be affected. Even under the new system it will still be advantageous to run an equine business on an agricultural holding, although the Rating Officer may attempt to differentiate between the two operations.

7 Yard management

Routines

Every yard should be so run that there is a happy and relaxed atmosphere in which horses can flourish. It is wisest to have a clear basic daily timetable which is adhered to, although hunting, competitions and other factors may necessitate a change. Horses will readily accept departures from the daily norm provided that there are routines within the timetable.

The timetables in this chapter are based on an eight hour working day. It is probable that the non-thoroughbred sector will soon follow the thoroughbred sector and other land-based industries so that a basic working week of 40 hours or so will became established. At present, in a great many yards the working week averages between 50 and 60 hours. In modern conditions this cannot really be justified although such owners maintain that the necessary work could not otherwise be done.

The timetables which follow show typical daily routines for three very different types of equine business.

Private, competition or livery yard

07.30 Give small hay feed, check signs of health, check rugs, check empty manger and water.
Muck out.
Give morning feed and leave horses in peace.
08.30 Breakfast. (If staff live out, they may arrive at 08.00 having had breakfast). Day's exercise list published.
09.00 Quarter all horses, pick out feet into a skip, put on day rugs and bandages (except horses on first exercise). Set fair the yard – everything tidy and in its place.
Tack-up first exercised horses.

09.30 First exercise.
       On return, allow the horses to roll and stale.
       Groom. (In some yards grooming is done in the afternoon but purists groom after exercise.)
       Rug-up.
11.15 Coffee and daily staff meeting.
11.30 Exercise second lot.
12.45 More hay; check water.
       Midday feed and leave horses in peace.
13.00 Lunch.
14.00 Exercise third lot.

Note: If grooming was deferred, all three lots of horses will have been exercised during the morning and grooming will be done now. By using a horse walker, or ride and lead, or by lunging and turning horses out in an exercise paddock, extra horses can be done or time saved to get other essential chores done.

15.30 Clean all tack and drink tea.
16.15 Put on night rugs, skip out, give hay, check water, set fair.
       Give evening feed and leave horses in peace.
17.00 Finish (could return from lunch at 14.30 and finish at 17.30).
21.00 Late check and any late feeds

This routine allows for considerable flexibility for the individual horses. The horses requiring the most time will usually be done in the first lot.

Riding school

08.00 Hay, water and feed.
08.15 Some staff muck out. Others fetch ponies from the fields and put them into stalls and groom them.
09.15 Set fair the yard and tack up for first ride.
       Those riding get changed.
09.30 First ride (working pupils).
       Exercise livery horses.
10.15 Prepare for second ride. Coffee.

Note: Throughout the day preparation for each ride starts 15 minutes in advance.

10.30 Second ride (fee-paying students). Other staff do yard chores. Those on first ride untack, brush off their horses and have coffee.

Note: After each ride all horses are untacked and brushed off throughout the day.

11.30 Third ride. (During term time this could be for 'senior citizens'.) Field and maintenance chores. Exercise remaining livery horses.
12.30 End of morning rides. School hired out.
       Midday stables.
13.00 Lunch.
14.00 Staff return from lunch. (Staff on evening duty have free afternoon.)
14.15 Fourth ride. This might be housewives with small children – provide creche.
15.15 Fifth ride.
       Tack cleaning. Tea.
16.15 Sixth ride.
17.15 Feed, hay and water. Put tack in readiness for evening rides.
17.30 High tea. School free for livery owners' use.
18.15 Evening staff on duty.
18.30 Seventh ride.
19.30 Eighth and final ride.
20.30 Night check and evening feeds.
20.45 Lock up.

In this routine all staff take 15 minutes off mid-morning and mid-afternoon and thus also work an 8 hour day.

Racing yard

06.00 Head lad only feeds and puts up exercise list.
07.00 Lads on yard. Muck out horses in first lot only, brush over, tack-up and tie-up.
       Put in hay and water but leave bed back.
07.45 First lot out for exercise
09.15 First lot back. Untack, brush over, pick out feet, set bed, rug up. Feed.
09.30 Lads' breakfast.
10.00 Lads on yard. Do second lot.
12.00 Second lot back, done over and fed.

12.30 Half the lads ride out the third lot (the sick, 'lame' and lazy). Remaining lads muck-out their stables and put their feeds ready.
13.15 Third lot back, done over and fed.
13.30 Lads go to lunch and yard is closed.
16.00 Lads return, skip-out and groom horses.
17.00 Trainer's inspection.
After inspection, each horse is rugged-up, hayed and watered.
17.45 Feed.
18.00 Finish.
21.00 Night check and fourth feed if necessary.

By having extra exercise riders, most of the horses go out on the first two lots but this may mean that several of the lads have to get two horses ready. The day's exercise list shows who will ride each horse at exercise.

Motivation and standards

The first two routines illustrated allow the staff opporunitites to use their initiative and skills as thinking riders, teachers and trainers. By giving staff responsibility they will be the more strongly motivated. However, staff should not be left to their own devices without guidance. Inexperienced staff rapidly become demoralised if faced with problems which they do not have the knowledge and experience to solve. The role of management is crucial in setting standards and motivating the team. Guidance, praise, good example and achievable targets stimulate staff to achieve more. The old-fashioned attitude that having paid for a day's work, one can expect a day's work, shows little appreciation of human nature.

Remuneration and benefits

Remuneration is the total reward for service, and includes not only the salary or wage, but the so-called 'fringe benefits' as well. If accommodation is provided, with or without board, staff will appreciate its value if they cost local charges. Board or part board may include use of laundry facilities and so on.

Riding tuition is also a valuable part of the overall remuneration, but by the same token a lesson missed is the equivalent of a deduction from wages. If employees are to appreciate the value of riding instruction, the lessons must be given as promised; the same applies to instruction in theory and examination practice. Keeping one's own horse at livery as part of the package is fairly easy for someone to cost – but a difficulty may arise if the individual thinks that the labour costs nothing if the work is done in free time. The only satisfactory way of dealing with this is to allow the individual to look after his own horse but to treat it as any other horse at livery, i.e. the time spent on looking after it is working time which could have been spent on a client's horse.

Allowing staff to use a vehicle for their own purposes can be a valuable perquisite, and it is worthwhile explaining to new staff the running costs involved. Too much must not, however, be made of such things. A safe guide for basic rates is the scale of agricultural wages.

Staff working an eight hour day might have one day off each week and one monthly weekend off. This is the quivalent of a five and a half day or 44-hour working week. Days off in lieu of Bank Holidays worked must be allowed for, as well as annual paid holidays. The total time off in a year might look like this:

	First year	Subsequent years
Holidays	14 days	21 days
Free weekends	24 days	24 days
In lieu of Bank Holidays	8 days	8 days
Days off	50 days	49 days
Total days off	96 days	102 days

In fact, allowing for sick leave, possible compassionate leave and days off for training, one might expect each member of staff to work an average of only 260 days in the year. In terms of staff numbers, an example may help: suppose the yard has a fairly level uptake of work throughout the year, and seven staff are needed on duty every day, the calculation to arrive at the staff needed by the business might be:

7 × 365 days = 2555 staff days
2555 staff days/260 days worked = 10 employees

Thus, if seven employees are needed on the yard each day, the business must employ ten people, and a flexible schedule must be worked out to enable each person to go on holiday. A sensible plan is to hold a staff meeting in January of each year to discuss holiday timing, and a year planner can then be displayed in the office to show the holidays and days off of all staff.

Daily duties

Apart from the daily routines, every equine business has days which are different whether because of regular occurrences such as the farrier's visit or a seasonal event like an Open Day. The staff need to know of these things in advance. Wall chart year planners, stocked by most stationers, offer an ideal solution. Self-adhesive labels of differing shapes and colours can be used to denote particular types of activity. Such a planner has already been suggested for staff holidays; a second one can be used to schedule anticipated happenings affecting the yard. Where a year planner is not adequate, then booking boards can be used.

Booking boards

Booking boards are suitable for a busy yard or training stable and for those with many engagements in competitions and so on. Their use and display enables the person answering the telephone to see engagements, deadlines, build-ups to major events and so on.

The recommended system requires two wipe-clean wall boards each permanently marked with a spirit-based pen into a seven column grid for the days of the week, and a cross marked into five columns to allow for the weeks in the month. In use, the first board would be the month of January, and the second the month of February. Information is written onto the grid using an erasable marker, i.e. a water based pen. At the end of January, all the essential information is copied into a log book as a permanent record. The board is then wiped clean with a damp cloth leaving only the grid, and the month of March is then marked in.

Using this system, there is at least one month ahead clearly on view. But the boards must be sited carefully next to the telephone, and the Head Lad or Yard Manager must check them each day.

Day work sheets

Pre-prepared day work sheets are a suitable aid to planning. The format will depend on the needs of the business but, once devised, they can be produced quickly and cheaply by any secretarial or printing agency.

Day work sheets can be used to show which horse will be ridden by whom. For example:

Day: Date:

Horse   1st lot   2nd lot   3rd lot

In a racing yard, the head lad might like to suggest a list, but the trainer checks it and makes the final decisions. The names of the horses in training are filled in in advance and so the trainer needs only to write the rider's name against each horse in one of the three columns. Blanks against a horse's name mean that it is off sick or away racing. The completed day work sheet is posted on the yard notice board first thing every morning.

A similar system used in some racing and schooling yards is based on a magnetic board, and so no writing is involved. Some schooling yards also use a different printed format:

Day: Date:

Horse   Start time   Duration   Type of work   Rider   Groom   Special attention

---

The horses' names can again be written down in advance. This system allows for individuality but is set against the basic daily timetable for the yard.

A riding school is the most complex in terms of a daily work sheet because each horse will work on several occasions. In the case of the suggested timetable, however, lessons are only held eight times. Allowing for a possible indoor school, outdoor school and a hack taking place at any one time, the corresponding daily work sheet could be: